Conte

Introduction

Ayubowan! If you have no idea what that means, this is a traditional Sri Lankan greeting, and it basically means hello, hi there, a wonderful greeting to a wonderful country.

You've picked up this book, and that basically means that you are either heading to Sri Lanka soon, and you want to know more about it, or you're thinking about it, and you're somewhat on

the fence. If you are in the latter category, hopefully this book will push you to get booking, because Sri Lanka is a country which packed with wonderful sights to see, amazing cultural experiences, nature and wildlife like nowhere else, and of course, some downright stunning beaches. Of course, that's not all this Indian Ocean island has to offer, because its long and interesting history also makes it somewhere to learn about too.

Originally called Ceylon, Sri Lanka is a country located in Southern Asia, which is just to the south

THAJ
236
NEW CITY FASHION
234

of India. Because of its location, you're getting an intoxicating melting pot of different cultures and influences, which all comes together to create a certain blend. Ask anyone who has visited Sri Lanka, and they will no doubt tell you that they are planning to go back, or already have done! One visit will leave you wanting more, but it's also important to make sure that you get to see everything you're wanting to in your first trip, just in case this is a once in a lifetime kind of deal for you.

This book aims to give you all the information you need when it comes to visiting this Indian Ocean gem. From where to stay, where to drink, where to eat, where to go, how to get there, how to get around, and plenty of background information, we leave no stone unturned, so you can certainly call this book your ultimate guide.

You won't need anything else, other than a strong sense of adventure, and desire to get out and see everything this beautiful destination has to offer.

Of course, you can't be expected to absorb every single piece of information and remember it whilst you're out and about, so read through our book, and then take it with you! You can dib in and out of when you need to, perhaps when you're free one evening and wondering where to eat, or perhaps you're trying to put together your itinerary of activities for the following day. We want to be your guiding light, your travel buddy, and your source of information.

When visiting a country such as Sri Lanka, somewhere with such a rich history and culture, it's important to throw yourself into it completely. These kinds of destinations are not for someone who doesn't want to explore, and just wants to sit on the beach. Whilst that kind of vacation is fine occasionally, if you're really wanting to have an experience, a true travel epiphany, then it's vital that you truly immerse yourself in everything that Sri Lanka has to offer.

Let's sum it up; let's give you a quick reference guide on what is so wonderful about this fantastic island:

- Sri Lanka is packed with culture and spirituality, which is easy to explore no matter whether you know much about it beforehand, or you don't
- The nature on the island is breath-taking, with countless natural parks to explore. You can camp, you can walk through the rainforest, you can trek, you can go on wildlife safari, basically you can do all manner of natural activities
- You can hike in Sri Lanka, yes really!
- Colombo is a city

which is packed with history and architecture to explore

- The food is divine!
- If you want to visit the underwater residents of the Indian Ocean, it's very easy to do in Sri Lanka!
- Elephants – that's all we need to say on that matter
- You can shop 'til you drop in Colombo, but also at the many traditional markets around the island
- There are several experiences to be had too, such as homestays with locals, outdoor adventures, wildlife watching, and learning all about Ayurvedic medicine
- Sri Lanka is a top destination for meditation retreats
- Honeymooners love Sri Lanka, because of the scenery
- But, you don't necessarily have to be a honeymooner to enjoy it!
- Visa rules might seem complicated at first, but they are actually very open and easy for everyone
- There is a huge range of accommodation on offer for everyone, including every budget
- If you want to go for super-luxury when it comes to your hotel, there are some of the most sophisticated choices available on the coastal resorts
- The heart of the country is Kandy, which is packed with nods to Buddhist spirituality – this is something you have to experience for yourself
- You can have all manner of different types of vacation here, from beach resorts to backpacking expeditions

Of course, we could sit and think of many more examples of why you should visit, but let's get to the real nitty-gritty of it, and learn all about this Indian Ocean gem.

So, without further ado, grab your explorer's hat, and let's get started!

Chapter 1: Sri Lanka 101

In order to really get the most out of any destination on this wonderful planet of ours, you need to know a bit about it before you head there. It's no good packing a suitcase, investing in some sun tan lotion that promises to give you a golden glow, grabbing your flip flops and heading off to the airport, expect-

ing some divine intervention to enlighten you as you jet over a full continent on your way there. If you are expecting this, you're going to be sorely disappointed!

No, in order to grab every single piece of fun and fascination out of any destination, you have to do your homework. Sri Lanka makes homework fun!

This chapter is going to serve as a full introduction. We mentioned in our introduction that this book is either for people who are going to be visiting Sri Lanka, or those who aren't sure, and the aim is that if you're not sure, this chap-

ter will be what swings your decision. We're going to talk about where Sri Lanka is, why it's so downright amazing, a bit about the history, the culture, the nature, and the wildlife, and we're also going to talk about the more spiritual side of the island too.

If reading about all of this doesn't grab your attention and your imagination, nothing else will!

Where is Sri Lanka, and Why is it so Great?

Of course, you need to know where it is you're going! We mentioned that Sri Lanka is lapped by those crystal clear waters of the Indian Ocean, and for many, that is one of the major pulls. Can you imagine waking up to the glittering of a translucent ocean every morning?

Sri Lanka is a Southern Asian country, which lies just off the Indian mainland. Simply because India isn't too far away, and South East Asia isn't too far away, you can imagine the sheer amount of influence that these countries have had on Sri Lanka itself. Whilst it maintains a lot of personality and independence, there's no doubt that its neighbours have rubbed off on it somehow. This is great news for visitors, because that really does give you a vibrant and varied experience.

The capital city is Colombo, and most visitors arrive at Colombo Bandaranayake International Airport from various cities around the world. Whilst not all of these flights are direct, the connection is usually not too far away, either in Singapore or Dubai as a general rule. You should certainly make the best use of a stopover in either of these cities if you're lucky enough! There are of course other stop off cities, such as Istanbul, Mumbai, or Abu Dhabi too.

So, we know where it is, and we know that you can fly there from lots of different places, but why is this country so downright amazing? Why should you drop everything and book right now?

I urge you to Google it, and turn your search to the images. You don't have to read the words, because that's our job to tell you, but in terms of pictures, just gaze upon them for a few minutes.

You want to go now, don't you?

Sri Lanka is a country which encompasses so much into its relative small size (65,610 square kilometres to be exact), that you will be very unlikely to be bored for even a single second. We're talking about history, culture, traditions, food, beach time, wildlife, nature, religion, spirituality, entertainment, is there anything else you could want? Oh yes, weather, there's some amazing weather to consider too. We'll talk about the climate and when the best time to visit is a little later in the book (the next chapter), but for now, just think sun, sun, sun, and you're not far wrong!

You can mix city life with rainforests, jungle treks with beaches, temples with markets, and nightlife with shopping. This is an island which really does tick a box for everyone, as cliché as that sounds!

Let's Get Historical

History doesn't have to be boring, because if you take the time to learn about the history of a place, you can understand it much more easily when you arrive. History shapes everything, from the way things are, to the way they will be, and

Sri Lanka has a lot more history than most places!

We have already mentioned that Sri Lanka used to be called Ceylon, until it gained independence from Great Britain in 1948, when plans were put into place to change the name to Sri Lanka; this finally happened in 1972.

The history of Sri Lanka goes right back to ancient India, when there are mentions of the island in texts written way back when. The island it thought to have been the site of King Ravana's fortress, before the Sinhalese people took over the island in the 6th century BC. At this time, the spiritual side of Sri Lanka began to take shape, as Buddhism was developed as the primary religion on the island.

Although several famous kingdoms took shape throughout ancient history, we move up to the 16th century when the Portuguese invaded, as well as the Dutch in the 17th century. We mentioned that Sri Lanka's neighbours have had a huge influence on the island, because of proximity, but because of history, you'll find Portuguese and Dutch influences too. Of course, Sri Lanka was long a part of the Great British Empire, from 1802, until 1948, when it won independence in its own right.

It's important to know all of this, not necessarily in the greatest detail, because you will see nods to history across the island, and knowing what they pertain to makes your experience more enriching. We can't however ignore the fact that Sri Lanka has had a troubled past throughout recent history, with fighting between the military government and the Tamil Tigers. This trouble raged from 1983 until 2009, and although conditions are certainly improved, there is still the odd flash point from time to time, usually in rural parts of the country, or the main capital city. We're going to cover safety in more detail later in the book, but it's worth mentioning that rural areas may be subject to occasional unexploded land mines. These are in the process of being cleared up by the Sri Lanka Army.

A Few Traditions And Customs You Should Experience

Towards the end of our book we will go over a few cultural issues you need to know, so you don't embarrass yourself, or anyone else, during your time in Sri Lanka. This particular section however is going to talk about the traditions and customs that you definitely need to experience, to help you have a much more enriching time on the island.

Sri Lanka is a very cultural island, and there are several sacred sites which are representative of the spiritual side of life here. There are several ancient towns and cities which have been preserved by UNESCO World Heritage Status, and these should be visited and respected, including the world famous sacred and ancient city of Kandy. Don't worry, we'll go into a little more detail on this later in the book, in what is called the Cultural Triangle.

In the cities, you will notice a slightly more western culture, however if you look closely, you will still see the thread of tradition running through daily life. Overall, Sri Lankan people are not impressed by opulence and wealth, living a relatively simple life. People are kind, generous, and hospitable; family is at the centre of everything. If you get the chance to

speak to a local family, do it, because you will learn so much about the way of life. Of course, if this is away from a tourist area, you may experience a language barrier, but you can still try and incorporate this into your trip in the tourist areas too.

Greetings

You will find that many people will greet you in a certain way, namely with their hands clasped together, and a nod of the head, with the word 'Ayubowan'. This is a traditional way of greeting those you know and those you don't know, and the words mean 'may you live long', which is basically 'hello' at the same time! If you are in a Tamil area, or with a Tamil family, the word will be 'Vanakkam', and a Muslim family will say 'Assalamu Alaikum'. You should try and do the same in response.

If you can try a learn a few words of the language (both of them) before you go, you will have a much more fulfilling time away. Of course, don't worry if you can't quite grasp the pronunciation straight away – nobody will expect for you to get it totally right the first time, or the second, or third! The point is that you're trying, and they will certainly appreciate your effort.

Dancing

Traditional Sri Lankan dance is also a must experience too. There are three main traditional types, namely the Kandyan dance, Low Country, and Sabaragamuwa. You'll find these performed mainly at weddings, celebrations, in homes, villages, and in temples, but if you visit a traditional entertainment evening, which is often found at large resorts, you will probably see this too. In this case, you should give it a go! You will have some fantastic memories, and hey, you'll have learnt something new!

Traditional Dress

Because of its close proximity to India, you will notice a lot of different types of clothing being worn in a traditional manner. For instance, you will have seen the sari in Indian culture, but you will also see it in Sri Lanka, worn at ceremonies and celebrations. Traditionally, the sari has six yards of cloth, usually brightly coloured, wrapped around the wearer several times over – watching someone put one on is quite the experience in itself – six yards is a lot of material! Depending on where you are in the country, and the beliefs of the wearer, the design will differ slightly. This is also one of the most popular things to buy in Sri Lanka also.

Aside from this, you'll also find the sarong. No, this is not what you wear to the beach, although the traditional form is where the modern style came from. This is actually printed or it can be plain and it is used to cover the wearer's legs, by wrapping around the waist. Men wear these more than women.

Finally, we have the diyareddha, and this is what you will see women wearing on the beach and in pools, as a traditional form of swimming costume. You'll also see women wearing this in villages, usually during the evening time, when they venture down to the rivers and lakes for a bath and a swim! This is almost like a sarong, i.e. it is a piece of material that comes under the arms and down to the knees, tied in a knot, or secured.

As with most countries these days, culture has been influenced by the west and by various other things, and this means that you won't always see the traditional types of dress, and in some cases you will see an adapted form, rather than the full-on described type. Sri Lanka has a large Muslim community, and this means that you will often see women with their heads covered, but you will also see Muslim women who don't cover their head – this is often personal choice, and down to the individual concerned.

Of course, with any type of cultural issue, you should give total respect,

avoid staring, and simply treat it as the norm, because that's exactly what it is.

Important Days

As with most countries around the world, Sri Lanka has several notable dates throughout the year. If you are visiting at this time, make sure you head to a celebration of some sort, as you're sure to be in for a real party, and probably plentiful free food! Sri Lankans love to party, and they know how to do it too!

As a side note, if we're talking about when to actually hold a celebration of

some sort, e.g. a wedding, for instance, then the Sri Lankans are certainly very big believers in asking the stars to help out. Astrology is a big thing here, and horoscopes are often called upon to find out if two lovers are actually compatible for marriage!

Again, locals will be more than happy to help you learn about this mystical custom, and if you show a genuine interest, you're sure to learn something new.

Full Moon Days

Every month when the full moon is high in the sky, this is a holiday day in Sri Lanka. On these days, you can't buy alcohol or meat anywhere. The official name for these days is Poya Days, and this is a religion day every month, pertaining to Buddhism. Many people will head to the temple on this day. Again, around this time you will notice more in the way of traditions, particularly traditional dress.

New Year (But Not January!)

Also known as Aluth Avurudda, the New Year is a big deal in Sri Lanka, however this is not when you would expect it to be, and actually usually lands some time in April. The actual date depends on

NDB bank

when astrology deems it to be time. During this celebration, you will find traditional foods passed around from family to family, and plentiful fun and frivolity, with traditional dancing too.

Of course, there are a few more important days of note, but these differ from year to year, so it will probably be a case of doing a little of your own research nearer to the time, to see if there are any particular days of note occurring during your visit.

Traditional & Alternative Medicine

Traditional medicine is THE big thing in Sri Lanka, and it is often preferred over regular medicine. Whether you go down this route or not, well, that's personal preference, but as a tradition, this is something that's certainly interesting to learn about.

Alternative medicine has been passed down through generations, and the first alternative medicine hospital was established as far back as the 4th century BC! If you venture towards the Cultural Triangle (more on that later), then you will see the ruins of these hospitals, which featured medicines which were natural in every sense, e.g. from the fruit and herbs of the land.

A Natural Country, Packed With Wildlife

Sri Lanka is a country that is packed, quite literally, with national parks and nature reserves. We're going to talk in more detail about these in our 'what to see' section, but the bottom line is if you're someone who loves the Great Outdoors, and someone who loves to have their jaw dropped by wildlife, basically this is the country for you.

There are several natural rainforests which you can easily visit, and this also means that you can visit the wildlife that reside here too. Bodhinagala Forest Reserve is one of the most popular, as it is actually set in an old Buddhist monastery. This rainforest is truly tropical and has some fantastic places to bird watch. On top of this you will be able to stop a few monkeys (quite mischievous, they are!), and you camp there too. Of course, Sri Lanka is also home to several elephant orphanages and sanctuaries, which are very popular pulls for tourists.

The native wildlife on the island includes those

majestic elephants that we all know and love, as well as many different species of monkey. You'll be able to spot manatees and dugongs, many different rodents, including the flying squirrel, bats, birds, whales, golden jackals, Sri Lankan leopards, deer, and donkeys, to name just a small selection. Of course, you can venture towards the coastline and spot some seriously impressive fish too.

Basically, we could talk about nature all day long, but without mentioning specific places to visit, which we're going to do in a later chapter, we could be talking for far too long! Put simply, Sri Lanka is an outdoor adventurer's dream, and if you love animals, you're going to be in your element.

The Spiritual Side of Sri Lanka

Sri Lanka is a mysterious, spiritual, and religious country, and if you don't explore this side of the island, you're missing out on an intrinsic part. It's best not to talk about religion with someone you don't know, because this being a sensitive subject, you don't want to cause offence. Buddhists, Christians, Muslims, and Hindus all live in peace in Sri Lanka.

Aside from religion, astrology, alternative medicine, meditation, are all very popular subjects, and they are a key part in the everyday life of islanders. Visiting a temple is something you simply have to do, and within the Cultural Triangle, you won't struggle to find a beautiful and peaceful temple to spend your time in. Remember to be respectful at all times, and again, we will cover this in more detail in a later chapter.

It's important to keep an open mind when visiting a country like Sri Lanka, because it's often the case that people with a very western mind are not as open to the practices and spiritual side of life, unlike the residents of this part of the world. If you allow yourself to learn, you will gain so much from your time on the island. Many people venture to Sri Lanka for meditation retreats, and it's very hard not to relax and focus your mind when you're surrounded by so much beauty! If you get the chance to do this, it's certainly a fantastic way to get away from it all, and perhaps find a little enlightenment of your own.

Basic Facts to Know

Consider this your quick go-to guide of basic facts to remember when visiting Sri Lanka.

Capital city Considered to be Colombo in terms of commercial means and tourism, although strictly speaking the official capital is Sri Jayewardenepura Kotte.

Money matters LKR – Sri Lankan Rupee. This is different to the Indian Rupee. You will be able to find ATMs in the major cities, however away from here it will always be cash.

Language There are two official languages of Sri Lanka; Sinhala is the main language, with more than half of residents speaking this language and also Tamil, which is also considered official, however only around 20% of the population speak this language. English is spoken in Sri Lanka, however not widely away from the main tourist areas.

Religion The main religion of Sri Lanka is Buddhism, with around 70% of the population within this bracket. Having said that, there are several other religions you will find in minority, including Hindu, Christian, and Muslim.

Time Zone GMT + 5.30 hours

Dialling code +94

Electricity issues In Sri Lanka you will find the UK-type of plug is used, i.e. three pin with 230V. If you are using a different type of appliance, you will need an adapter.

This chapter is an overview of what you need to know about Sri Lanka, but by no means and exhaustive guide! We just want to show you the basics, what you can expect, and hopefully it will have grabbed your attention enough to seriously considering pressing the 'book' button on that next vacation!

Of course, Sri Lanka is an island which has several destinations within it, and that means you either need to decide where to base yourself, or you need to plan your route to give you a complete experience. This is something which shouldn't be rushed, so make sure you read all about the main destinations in our next chapter, so you can complete your vacation without missing anything out!

Chapter Two: Sri Lanka's Best Destinations, And The Weather

Now we know how wonderful Sri Lanka is, we need to know when to go. Why? Because there is a slight issue to deal with – monsoon season.

This chapter is going to give you some ideas on the particular regions to go to, but also about the weather – two very important sections!

First things first, let's talk sun and rain.

Before we being, don't be put off by the R word. Yes, we know that you probably get enough of the wet stuff back home, which is partly why you're probably trying to escape to a sun-drenched island. Despite all of that, Sri Lanka is open to rain at almost any time, but this is short-lived on a lot of occasions, and when it's not, you're forewarned. You're unlikely to have a total washout, put it that way.

Now, monsoon season does not mean a total downpour lasting for an entire season, it means periodic rain across a season, and it's very important to understand these issues in terms of deciding when to go, and where to go too.

Weather Issues in Sri Lanka

The reason we are putting these two subjects together into one chapter is because the weather changes as you move around the island. Sri Lanka is shaped like a pear, and in the central region, towards the south, you will find more in the way of mountains; the higher you go, the more altitude you experience, the colder or wetter it can be. On the other hand, the coastline and the rest of the island experiences hot weather in abundance.

This is an island you'll need a hat and suntan lotion for! Being ready for every eventuality will serve you well, and that way you're never caught out!

The weather is warm because of the waters that surround it – namely, the Indian Ocean. The average temperature is warmer on the north-eastern coastline than it is in the mountains, by quite a drastic amount, regardless of the month. The hottest part of the island is on the north-eastern coast, namely in a town called Trincomalee – if you like heat, go here! During the hottest peaks in temperature, you can easily experience mercury which exceeds the 40s, so always remember to seek out as much shade as possible, and to make plentiful use of your hotel's air conditioning!

What we do need to address however is that pesky thing called monsoon season. It's not as complicated as you may think, and you basically need to correlate the distance, with the particular monsoon season.

Sri Lanka doesn't have the four seasons, instead it has two – wet season and dry season. Wet season is referred to as monsoon season. Within this, there are two monsoon seasons, which affect particular parts at different times. We need to talk about this because each monsoon season really does affect various parts of the island in different ways, and unless you want to be caught up in a torrential downpour, it's best to know when the ideal time to visit is. Again, remember, you're not going to experience a total washout! It's highly unlikely!

To further complicate matters, each part of the island has a dry season and a wet season in total correlation to the other part of the island. Confused? Let's explain a little, to help you make a more informed decision.

The North-Eastern Monsoon

From October to February the island experiences the north-eastern monsoon.

The island is most affected in the north-eastern region, hence the name, and this is also where one of the most popular destinations of the island lies – Kandy. During these months, you can expect a considerable amount of rain, quite unpredictably. As you head south, the rains taper off slightly, as the mountains act as protection during this particular monsoon.

Kandy is actually the part of the island during this time that gets the most precipitation, which is a bit of a pain when you consider that this is one of the most go-to parts. Despite that, the rain can be a refreshing change from hot temperatures, and you simply need to head out between downpours, or simply embrace the wet stuff!

On the other hand, Colombo is basically unaffected by either monsoon, because it rains the same amount in each season. It's worth knowing however that

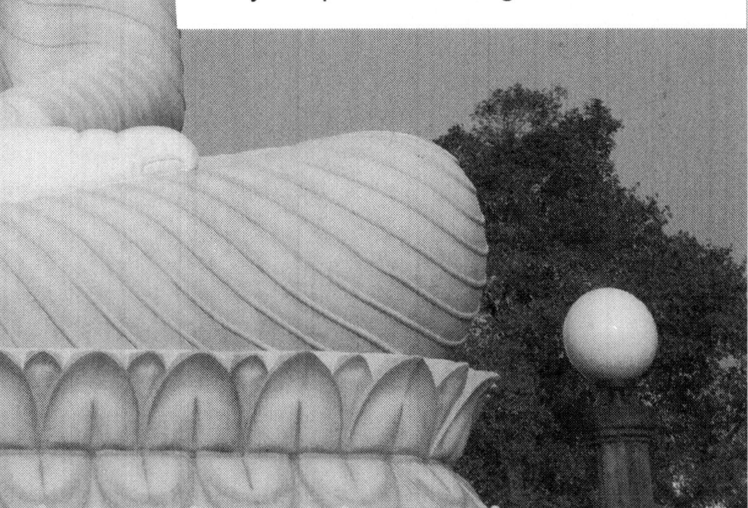

this particular monsoon is when temperatures across the island are a bit lower, so if you don't like stifling heat, this could be the ideal time to venture there. When visiting Colombo, the slight rain can actually be a blessing, because this is a busy and bustling city, and high temperatures and excessive sun do not make for a comfortable city exploration!

The South-Western Monsoon

From May to August, the island experiences the opposite monsoon, and this means that the other half of the island is affected, giving the north and north-east a little respite. Ratnapura is the place which is most affected by rains at this time.

Many of the island's top tourist attractions and nature reserves lie in the south, and this particular monsoon brings much needed liquid to the thirsty landscapes. It's actually interesting to see the lush vegetation grow greener before your eyes, and you may also see much more wildlife just before the wet season comes, because they will be more visible around shrinking waterholes in national parks.

The In-Between Times

February to May, and August to October are times when neither monsoon is in place, but that doesn't mean it can't rain. This is an island which is surrounded by water, and whilst the region is typically warm and sunny, oceans have weather systems which swirl around the, bringing unpredictable conditions from time to time. Sri Lanka can also occasionally experience adverse weather in the form of a cyclone, or typhoon, and this is ba-

sically a band of stormy weather, which will be very well predicted, have a very clear predicted path ahead of time, and will probably pass just as quickly as it comes. In these cases, simply heed advice from your hotel staff in terms of when it's best not to go outside, e.g. winds, and when it passes, you can easily get yourself back out there again and continue on with your vacation! This type of weather system is much more likely to affect the coastal regions, particularly the east and south coasts, because they are so open the weather affecting their neighbouring countries.

Again let's stress it some more - we might be pictur-

ing Sri Lanka as a rainy kind of destination, but that's really not the case! Rain, when it comes, can be very sharp, but it can also be very short-lived, leaving behind sunny conditions. The rain is often welcomed, because it can provide a little relief from the heat, and provided you keep an umbrella or a rain-mac (lightweight of course) in your bag, you're unlikely to experience a total wash-out.

It's really about planning your trip, according to where you want to go, around the monsoon seasons, or perhaps embracing the latter end of them, or right at the beginning. Again, you'll get lower temperatures, and that

can sometimes be a very major blessing if you're not a heat fan!

Sri Lanka's Provinces

Okay, so we know that the weather can be complicated, but we've also established that it doesn't matter, because Sri Lanka is amazing! Of course, where to go is going to be at the forefront of your mind, so let's outline the island a little and give you a few ideas. Bear in mind that when we mentioned specific towns, attractions,

and sights, we are going to talk about these in much more detail a little later on, so this chapter is really to give you an idea of how much there is to see in each part of the island.
It's also important to point out that we can't give you information on every single attraction, in every single town, on every single part of the island – we don't have paper or ink for that, or typing space anyway.
For now, let's just focus on the main big-hitters, and you can explore on your own steam to find a few extra hidden gems – hey,

you could even tell us about them!

Central Province

This region encompasses some of the most popular and most visited areas, including Kandy. This is the highest part of the island and you will find those famous tea plantations here. There are also some beautiful waterfalls and valleys to check out, and high-standing temples which are enough to make your eyes water with delight. Piduruthalaga, the highest mountain on the island, is within this region, providing protection to either side of the island during the opposite monsoon seasons, and World's End, the biggest cliff drop you'll probably ever see.

On top of this, you will find a few nature reserves, and plentiful camping opportunities. If you are a wilderness fan, getting out and enjoying a few nights under the stars is a must do. You don't have to rough it, so to speak, as there are some glamping opportunities too, and we'll mention a few of those as we get onto our accommodation section a little later on.

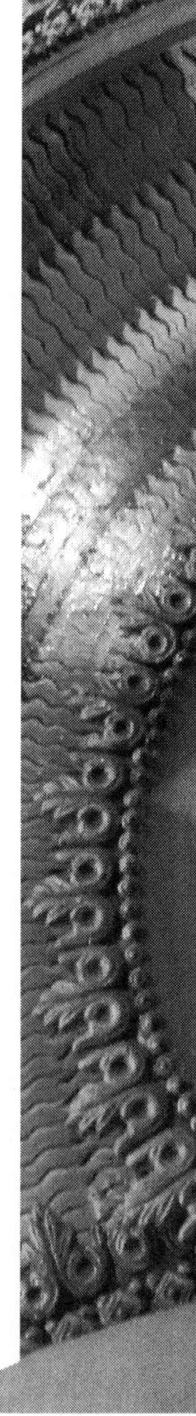

Northern Province

The far north of the island is not really the most well known in terms of tourism,

but it is starting to grow. This is because this region was badly hit by the civil war, and there are a few unexploded land mines still present. Whilst the army are doing their best to clear these up, this is a work in process currently. When this is completed, the area around Jaffna, furthest north, will undoubtedly be back to its former glory, with some of the hottest temperatures and beautiful beaches.

Landmine-risk areas are generally very well marked out, with signs giving you

advice to avoid. Now, this isn't the case everywhere, so it's always best to avoid roaming into rural land or roadsides, and to stick to marked paths. If you can do this, you should have a very uneventful time in this very beautiful part of the island.

North Central Province

If you love history, this is a province for you! Ancient history drips from every corner here, with the ancient and royal kingdoms based in this part of the island, back in the day. This is the Cultural Triangle we keep talking about, because of how much historical importance is present, and you can easily visit this part of the island, before venturing a little south into the Central Province, and heading to Kandy. You often find that the two regions, the central part and this part, are lumped together when talking about tourism, because they are so interchangeable – this is great news for explorers!

In the North Central Province however, you will find Anuradhapura, Polonnaruwa, Sigiriya, Dambulla, and Mihintale. This means plentiful

nature, and Sigiriya is a definite must visit in this region.

Eastern Province

Love beaches? This is your area! Trincomalee and Arugam Bay are located here, and these are very popular resorts, with stunning beaches to sit, relax, and basically forget all your care and worries. This is where you will find those iconic bungalows over the sea, the swaying palms, and the basic castaway vibe you've probably been looking for.

Surfing is also very popular here, and it's a

great sight to see, even if you aren't an experienced surfer yourself. Remember that riptides can be dangerous and unpredictable, especially at Arugam Bay, so never venture out into the water at high tide, or when you are warned not to. It's always best to keep your wits about you when it comes to this body of water. Despite that, you can look forward to some seriously beautiful, castaway beaches to enjoy.

North Western Province

This area is the one for wildlife lovers, and is also home to the largest national park, namely Wilpattu National Park. You can do plentiful dolphin and even whale spotting from this region, specifically in Kalpitiya.

If you love to spot wildlife, and perhaps even dream of going on safari, then this particular region should make an appearance on your trip. Whether you base yourself here, or you simply venture to this part as a section of your break, make sure it is on your itinerary.

Sabaragamuwa

This is the region where you will find the town of Ratnapura, but you will also find natural beauty in abundance. There are countless dramatic waterfalls, rainforests, plains and sights around here, as well as Adam's Peak. Checking out this wonder of nature, as well as a very important sacred spot, at sunset and sunrise is a

truly breath-taking sight, and you will find many excursions take this into account, which we will talk about a little later on.

Southern Province

This is another area for history lovers, but it is also a good place to head

for wildlife fans too. You will find the city of Galle here, which has plenty of history and architecture to explore, as well as several national parks, with lush rainforests and plentiful wildlife to check out.

This region also encompasses Weligama, Matara, Tangalle, Unawatuna,

Hambantota, and Yala National Park.

Yala National Park is one of the most famous, and because of its close proximity to Galle, you can easily do a nature and town break, with history thrown in for good measure, as well as a few beach days too. This probably the most all-rounder part of the island on the whole.

Uva

If you opt for a meditation or spirituality retreat, it's likely that you will be visiting this particular part of the country. This is one of the coolest parts, because of the altitude, with several retreats high up in the hills, with stunning views to check out. In a setting like this, it's impossible not to chill out!

We have to mention that the retreats in this part of the island do come at a price, but if you're keen

to enjoy the benefits of this mind, body, and soul experience, price shouldn't really come into it, right?

Western Province

Finally, we have another very popular part of the country to visit, because

this is the part where you will find Colombo. There are some other big cities in this region, as well as some fantastic beach resorts too. You will find Sri Jayewardenepura here, the 'other' capital city, Beruwela, Gampaha, and Negombo.

Colombo is a city that you definitely have a spend a day or two in, and there are many ways to explore it. We will talk a little later about the specifics on what you can see and do, but the open top bus tour is a good option. As cliché as it sounds, this is a fantastic way to really

check out a lot of things, in a very short space of time; if you're only going for the day, trying to cram as much in as possible is a must do, before you head back to your base resort, away from the hustle and bustle.

Sri Lanka's Cities

We've talked about the island as a whole, and we've split it up into the various official provinces, giving you an idea of where to visit and when, according to the weather, but what about city break lovers? You might not think of laid back Sri Lanka as somewhere to go to appreciate a full on city experience, but Colombo is certainly a vibrant place to head, and will give you a modern experience, with an old-fashioned twist.

Most of us love a day or two in a big city, and it's a great idea to combine beach, wildlife and city time into one vacation. Whilst most of Sri Lanka's cities are not huge, sprawling metropolis', they do have plentiful entertainment, shopping, and culture to explore, to give you that city hit you're looking for.

The main cities are:

- Colombo – The 'capital' in terms of commercial and business issues
- Batticaloa – You will find this city as a gateway to some fantastic beach resorts along the Eastern Province. Trincomalee is close by.
- Galle – A very historic place to visit, Galle has a Dutch fort still very well preserved, and is also an interesting city in its own right.
- Kandy – We're going to cover Kandy in much more detail, but it's proximity in the centre of the country means it is the real heart of the island. If

you're looking for spirituality, this is the place to go.

- Nuwara Eliya – Those seeking cool temperatures need to head into the hills to Nuwara Eliya, with some beautiful tea plantations, in calm surroundings.
- Ratnapura – This city is known as the City of Gems, and is a great spot for learning about everyday life.
- Jaffna – This is the most northern part of the island, and offers beautiful beaches and traditions to explore.

This chapter is designed to give you an overview of the different regions of Sri Lanka, and to highlight the size, including the weather issues that you need to keep in your mind. Again let's stress it once more

- remember, we are not describing this island as rainy! We simply need to inform you of the particular weather systems that can affect the island at certain times – nothing is set in stone! Whether it rains or not, you're unlikely to be at all disappointed with your time on the island, or the weather overall!

In our next chapter, we're going to talk about how to get around the island, the best way to see it, how to actually get in to Sri Lanka, and how you can see other countries around it, by being a true adventurer!

Hold onto your hats, we're going to get into great detail!

Chapter 3: The Best Ways to See Sri Lanka

There are three main ways to see Sri Lanka; the first is to base yourself in one particular destination and explore it to the max, perhaps having a few day trips out to other parts of the island (highly recom-

mended), the second is to travel around the island, e.g. backpacking, and the third is to visit from a neighbouring country, and to perhaps just see certain parts, e.g. your particular areas of interest.

All of these ways have their own advantages and disadvantages.

Let's explore this, so you can decide your own personal way to see this beautiful island.

Basing Yourself in One Destination

This would be the traditional type of vacation, e.g. you find one particular destination that you like the look of, and you book a hotel in that place, and explore it completely during your week or two (or maybe even more). Within this, as we just mentioned, you can take excursions out to various nearby attractions, either on your own steam, or as part of an organised tour.

This type of vacation is best suited to those who aren't so confident in terms of independent travel, because it gives you the chance to see interesting parts of the island, but you don't have to worry about how you're going to get around yourself.

Advantages

- You can totally relax, without having to think about where you're going next, and how you're going to get there
- You can see the destination you're basing yourself in completely, immersing yourself completely
- You can visit nearby attractions with a tour or by yourself, depending on how comfortable you feel with either option
- You will probably have all the perks of tourism at your fingertips, and that can be a real perk and safety net

Disadvantages

- You are going to be missing out on the adventure part of visiting Sri Lanka, and this really is something which should be explored if at all possible
- There are countless attractions and destinations to see, not just one area
- In order to say you have 'done' Sri Lanka, you'll need to return, which is costly and time consuming – not something we can all do, or afford!

Travelling Around Sri Lanka (Backpacking)

Next, we have a more adventurous type of vacation, and this is when you travel around the island at your own leisure. This can be either as part of an organised itinerary, or it can be basically that you make it up as you go along, but either way, you are seeing most of the island, if not all of it, over a set amount of time.

This doesn't have to be

backpacking, but we have lumped this together under that term, because backpacking is without a doubt the best way to see any destination on the planet freely.

Advantages

- You will be able to experience Sri Lanka totally, in the way you want to, seeing exactly what you desire
- You will also be able to learn about the history, the culture, traditions, and probably about the language much more easily and freely
- You're likely to meet a lot of new people along the way, some of

whom may become friends for life, as well as being able to gleam travel information gems from them

- You will gain a true sense of confidence from your adventure, and that is a really enriching experience
- You can design your trip to suit your own interests and preferences, without being stuck in one particular destination, with wanderlust on your mind

Disadvantages

- This type of vacation is not suited to anyone who is lacking in confidence in terms of travel
- You may not feel that you are relaxing, as you are always on the go, always needing to know how to get to your next destination
- A backpacking break of any kind means you need to be very careful when budgeting your cash, which can be stressful and distracting
- There are a few safety issues to take into account, and you always need to be on the lookout for up to date news going on in the region

Visiting Sri Lanka From a Neighbouring Country

Of course, you could head over to Sri Lanka for a few days or a few weeks as part of a break in another country, or countries. There are several countries with border Sri Lanka over the ocean, and that means that you can easily make your break a twin centre type of deal. There are visa issues to take into account here, but this is entirely possible if you cover all bases.

The countries around Sri Lanka are subtly different in their own right, so you certainly won't be getting 'same for same'.

Advantages

- You can truly say you have explored and entire region!
- You will be able to see the differences between Sri Lankan culture and the culture of its neighbours, showing you the subtle changes
- Heading over to the island from a nearby country is much cheaper than visiting independently, without the costly long-haul flying issue to take into account

Disadvantages

- There are likely to be visa requirements that you will need to research and meet, to avoid any problems on arrival or departure – this is something you will need to clue yourself up on before you go, and to stay updated on at all times
- Extra travel as part of your break may be something you don't like, and may take up precious sightseeing time
- You may fall in love with Sri Lanka and wish you had gone there for the entire break instead!

From this advantages and disadvantages list, you can see which type of travel is best suited to you and your needs, as well as your personality. Backpacking isn't for everyone, but then staying in one particular destination isn't for everyone either. Travel is a totally personal deal, which is what makes it so wonderful. Take the time to figure out which is the best way for you, so you can really explore Sri Lanka to the maximum. If you're still not sure, try speaking to other travellers, and gain some personal perspective.

How to Get to Sri Lanka in The First Place!

We mentioned in our first section of this book about travelling to Sri Lanka be-

ing much easier than it has ever been before, because of easy links from nearby countries, as well as a few direct flights. You need to know a little more than a brief mention however, so let's cover that now.

It's worth pointing out here that there are visa requirements, and we are going to cover those in a lot more detail later on, to make sure that you don't miss anything important out of your travel arrangements.

First things first however, how do you get to Sri Lanka in the first place?

Obviously, the most common way is to fly, however you can visit by boat also.

Let's cover air travel first.

Travelling to Sri Lanka by Plane

Colombo Bandaranayake International Airport (CMB) is the airport you will arrive at, and that means you can spend a day or two exploring Colombo itself, or you can venture back at some point during your break. Flights into the airport are much more plentiful than ever before, and whilst not all are direct, connections are plentiful, including many across Europe too.

The most common airline which flies into Sri Lanka is Sri Lankan Airlines, which as the name would suggest, is the national airline. The largest selection of flights are available through this carrier, including flights from across Europe, South East Asia, Middle East, China, Japan, India, and Pakistan. You can also link to neighbouring countries with this airline, and vice versa.

Emirates and Ethiad Airways are the two other big named carriers which serve Sri Lanka, although these are not direct and are connected via either Abu Dhabi, Dubai, or Singapore. If you have a stop over, make the most of it! The airports in these major connection hubs are packed with entertainment options, or you could head out and see the sights if you have a particularly lengthy stop over.

Sri Lankan Airlines, Emirates, and Ethiad Airways are the most frequent fliers to the island, but Qatar Airways has a few services a week, connecting in Doha; Singapore Airlines flies from Singapore daily, Turkish Airlines connects from Istanbul every day, Jet Airways has several flights operating from Mumbai and Bangalore, and Air Asia has several flights from Kuala Lumpur, which are often quite low in cost.

All the time there are new routes being added, so it's a case of checking the up to date options when you're thinking of flying, but overall, these are the main tried and tested routes which operate on a regular basis towards the island. Obviously, the nearer you are to Sri Lanka, the cheaper the flight cost, but you can often find low cost deals if you're a little savvy with your searching – try these options:

- Book your flights separately, e.g. your inbound flight and your outbound flight separately
- Use flight comparison sites to find deals;

its often the case that flying with one airline to Sri Lanka, and another on the way back, can yield cheaper results

- Indirect flights, e.g. connections, will always be cheaper than any direct flight you can find
- Can you travel with just hand luggage? It's unlikely if you're visiting for a long time, but if you're not, find an airline which has a generous hand luggage allowance, and be very careful with what you pack, buying your toiletries at the airport and wearing your heaviest items, e.g. shoes
- Make use of any airmiles you might have
- Book at the last minute
- Avoid those costly added extras, such as seat selection or additional meals

Saving a little cash on your travels will mean that you have more to spend when you're there.

Travelling to Sri Lanka by Boat

There did used to be several ferry services which ran between neighbouring countries and Sri Lanka, but these have currently been suspended, with no date given for their recommencement. Obviously, if this is a way to travel that you would prefer, just keep an eye on any news that may be announced at any time. Another option however, is via a cruise.

Whilst Sri Lanka isn't a massive cruise ship destination, it is growing in that regard, so look out for any cruise vacations that head to the island. This could give you a real 'try before you buy' kind of feel, because you can check it out for a day or two, and then decide whether to go back or not. Of course, we are biased, so we will certainly say that you'll be returning!

Cruises typically dock in

Trincomalee and Hambantota.

When you're travelling to and from neighbouring countries, e.g. backpacking or simply heading to another destination for a few days, this will almost always be by air.

How to Get Around Sri Lanka

Now we've covered how to actually get into Sri Lanka in the first place, we need to know how to get around and explore this wonderful island! Luckily, there are several options, you just need to pick the best one for you.

The options you have are:

- Bus
- Train
- Plane
- Taxi (car or Tuk-Tuk)
- Organised trip
- Self-drive (car or motorbike)
- Hiring a Tuk-Tuk

Travelling by Bus

Bus is the cheapest way to travel around the island, and it is probably the easiest way too, because there are plentiful services, no matter where you want to go (within reason). Just outside the airport you will find a shuttle bus service which takes you into Colombo, and from there the main bus service will take you wherever you want to go.

Typically, there are different standards of bus you can take, and the most basic (the cheapest) can be crowded and hot at certain times of the day. If you can stand this however, it is a very cheap way to get around. There are air conditioned buses, but these typically cost a little more, yet still cheap enough – you are also certain to get a seat on these buses,

which is not the case on the most basic ones!

The Government-run buses are called Lanka Ashok Leyland and they are red in colour. These cover the entire island. If you see a bus which is blue, these are still high quality and cheap, although privately owned. The minimum charge for buses on the island is LKR 9.

In order to catch the bus, you either head to the bus station, which is a much more organised affair, or you should flag the bus down on the road, just like you would do with a taxi. Once on the bus, you pay the conductor, who will give you a ticket, and

you take a seat, if you can find one. When you want to get off, either ring the bell (if you can get to it), or just tell the conductor – whilst they may not speak English, hand signals or a few broken words will certainly do the job.

If you're not too keen on the idea of a local bus, and you want something a little more luxurious, particularly good if you're travelling from one end of the island to another, then you can opt for the air conditioned buses, or a super luxury bus. These are more expensive, however you get the seat and you get air conditioning, which may be worth the extra cost!

Air conditioned buses have their destination displayed in green, and although there is less room for luggage on these buses, you will have a much more leisurely journey. Alternatively, super luxury buses are less common, but much more comfortable. Bear in mind that you will pay considerably more for these buses, so it's a good idea to question how much luxury you really need! It's a good idea to pre-book these particular buses, particularly the overnight options. A word of warning however – if your bus stops for a break, make sure you're back on the bus ahead of time, because they don't tend to do a head count, and you might find yourself stuck!

Travelling by Train

One of the best ways to check out the passing scenery is to travel by train. This is a real adventure, yet a comfortable one. Certain trains also have observation sections, so you can get a really good view of what is passing you by.

Now, the downside of a train is that it can sometimes be a slower option, but the good news is that it is sometimes (quite commonly) cheaper than going by bus. Trains can be crowded at certain times of the day, especially around big towns and cities during commuter times, and if you want to sit in the observation section, it's a good idea to book ahead of time. You can check online for train times, to give you a better idea of where you can go and how easily.

As with most countries, there are different seating classes available, including first class, second class, and third class, with the price increasing and decreasing in each direction.

Basically, if you like scenery (and who doesn't), then train travel is the way to go. Some of the most breathtaking scenery will pass you by, and not at a speed where you won't catch it! The mountain areas are simply divine and if you're not planning on visiting them and stopping off yourself, travelling through them can offer the perfect sense of middle ground. One common tip is to try and sit on the right of the train carriage if at all possible, as this is thought to give you an even more picturesque view.

If you're torn between the experience and the views, and the idea you have in your head of people hanging out of the train because it's so crowded, be assured that train travel in Sri Lanka is rarely as packed as you may see in the big Indian cities. Yes, it can be crowded, but if you can avoid peak times, e.g. late afternoon and early morning, then you won't have any issues. Also, it's a good idea to book a higher class, and then you will be guaranteed your seat.

Travelling by Plane inside Sri Lanka

Yes, this island might not be as massive as some you might be thinking of, but it's still large enough to mean that you can take a small seaplane from one end to the other! This is a great option if you're in a rush, or you don't want to waste time actually travelling from A to B. Obviously, this is the most costly option we have mentioned so far, but it does have its advantages, namely that they never get that high into the sky so you really get to see everything clearly.

The seaplanes are operated by the national airline, and they run to most of the big destinations on the island, including Kandy.

Travelling by Taxi or Tuk-Tuk Taxi

If you're trying to get around a large town or city, particularly Colombo, then a taxi is a good idea, and can work out to be quite cheap too, for shorter distances. Taxis work by the meter, so you know that you're not being overcharged, whilst you can, with some taxi companies, set up a day package, which allows you to dib in and out of using your taxi throughout the day, for a set charge.

You can use Uber on the island nowadays, including UberX and UberGo. Bear in mind that this is usually more expensive than a taxi, but does offer you a more comfortable experience.

Now, a Tuk-Tuk on the other hand can cost a little more than a regular car taxi, but it can also be a true experience! It's not like you can experience this type of vehicle in all countries across the planet, so perhaps even if you only do it once, you should!

If you have no idea what a Tuk-Tuk is, this is basically a three wheeled vehicle, and the name comes from the noise they make when the horn is blasted. Do bear in mind that they don't have seat belts or doors, so if you're super-safety conscious, you might not enjoy the experience that much!

You won't struggle to find a Tuk-Tuk, and you simply flag it down like you would a taxi in the street. These are metered and non-metered, but it's always best to try and get a metered option if possible, to avoid being scammed or paying much more than you should. Rates do vary.

Travelling by Organised Trip

There are now many tour operators who have set itineraries to take you across the main sights of the island, and it's really a case of finding a company with an itinerary that suits you. Some of the most reputable and large tour operators include:

- Walkers Tours
- Aitkenspence Travels
- Ceylon Tours
- Ceylon Routes Sri Lanka
- Tangerine Tours
- JF Tours
- Rameca Travel and Leisure
- Dilhan's Awesome Adventures

There are countless more, but remember to check out ratings and accreditation, before parting with any cash.

Self-Drive Options

The most independent way to see the country is obviously by driving your own car, and you have three main rental options here:

- Car
- Tuk-Tuk
- Motorbike

It's certainly true that the last two options are not for the faint-hearted, but overall, this is one of the best ways to really experience everything the island has to offer. You can easily stop off whenever you want, design your own itinerary, and take your time, without having to rush to a public transport schedule, or one which a tour operator designs for you. The downside is of course that you are driving in a foreign country, which has different rules to what you are likely to be used to – we are going to cover that in our next section, to help you see what you can and can't do.

Hiring a car isn't difficult, especially in Colombo, where there are countless hire companies on hand to try. Cars work out cheaper than Tuk-Tuks, mainly because of the novelty value, and are no doubt safer too. You can hire a car with a driver, if you don't want to do the driving yourself, although this is more expensive, or you can self-drive and go on your own steam. It's likely that you will need to leave a deposit of cash at the centre before you head off towards the horizon, and always check that insurance is included in the deal.

If you're wanting to hire a motorcycle, you will need to have a motorcycle licence in the first place, and you should always wear your helmet. Headlights should be kept on at all times, even in the day, and bear in mind that you cannot drive a motorcycle which is in excess of 250cc on any public road.

Alternatively, if you want to go down the route of hiring a Tuk-Tuk, be prepared to pay a little extra. It's never a good idea to arrange to rent a Tuk-Tuk from an owner, because you never know what you're getting, and instead use a reputable middle-man service, such as Tuk Tuk Rental Sri Lanka, who will do all the checking out ahead of time for you.

Advice on Driving in Sri Lanka

Remember the following points:

- Drive on the left hand side
- You will need to obtain an international Driving Permit before you travel, and a Sri Lankan recognition permit also, which can be obtained in Colombo, or your hire company will be able to advise you on the nearest centre for you to do this. In addition, you need to keep your own driving licence with you at all times too, your passport, insurance documents, visa paperwork (if necessary), and any other important travel documentation you may have
- If you are hiring a motorbike, you will need to have an existing motorcycle licence, third party insurance, and helmets are to be worn at all times, without exceptions
- Only drive if you are confident that you can do it, and you are experienced – conditions in big towns and cities can be somewhat crazy. Whilst there are rules of the road in general, nobody really abides by them
- Always give way to larger vehicles – whilst there are set rules, not everyone seems to abide by them
- If you hear some-

one sounding their horn, this is an indication that they are coming up behind you, in front of you, etc, and you should be aware – it is not a sign of aggression, like in some countries!

- The terrain varies from place to place, so always heed warnings, especially in the mountainous regions, where roads can be steep and narrow
- If you are venturing into the central area, or perhaps the mountains in general, it's probably best to hire a 4x4, to ensure you make up and back down those hills with your car full
- Always be on the lookout for hazards, but even more so than normal – whether you're in a city, town, or rural area, it's not unusual for a random animal to jump out or trot along beside you, and it's often the case that Tuk-Tuks simply drive however they like!

Driving in Sri Lanka is an experience, and it is something you should certainly only do if you are confident and alert. Having said that, it is certainly the best way to see this beautiful island, and to have a real experience at the same time.

Okay, so we've covered how to get to the island and how to get around it, but now it's time to get onto the good stuff! What can you see in Sri Lanka? Let's explore!

Chapter 4: What to See And Do in Sri Lanka

It's time for the fun stuff! We're going to talk about the most famous attractions you can visit in Sri Lanka now, as well as a few lesser known ones, to really enrich your time away. Of course, it's not just sights you can see, but experiences you can have too, and we'll cover those as well.

By no means could we possibly give you an exhaustive list, because there's far too much to mention, but by highlighting the main areas, and making sure you know the best spots to visit, you can certainly make sure you get the most out of your time on the island. If you're only visiting for a short time, e.g. a two week long vacation, you should pick the attractions and experiences which are close to where you are basing yourself, and if you're backpacking around, you have much more free rein – lucky you!

It's a good idea to draw up a rough itinerary, so you don't miss out on things. When we are away on vacation, it's so easy to be leisurely, and whilst that is perfectly fine, if you spend all morning lazing around, having a long breakfast, and trying to decide what to do, before you know it, half the day is gone, and you could have been out seeing something amazing. We're not talking about having a clipboard itinerary with you, which must be rigidly adhered to, but instead a rough idea of where you might want to go on a certain day. For instance, if there is a show on at an attraction on a Monday, and you really want to see it, obviously you need to go there on a Monday. It's not rocket science!

Now, as a quick mention, we aren't going to cover beaches in this particular section, because we're going to dedicate a whole chapter to Sri Lanka's beautiful beaches very shortly. For now, let's focus on what you can get up to!

Wildlife Attractions & Experiences

There are countless wildlife sanctuaries and national parks in Sri Lanka, and the hardest part is really whittling it down to which one you want to visit. There are vacations you can take where you actually stay in the jungle or rainforest, in eco-friendly huts, and these are often arranged and guided by an adventure vacation company. If this is something you're interested in, it's a good idea to book directly with such a company, so you know that everything is covered, e.g. insurance etc.

Below you will find a selection of the best wildlife parks to venture to during your stay.

Yala National Park

This is the island's most famous park, and the most visited too, so you can expect crowds during the busier times of the year. The park is famous for its leopards, and there are many of them!

Yala National Park is located around six hours south from Colombo, near to Tissamaharama and Kirinda. This is a jeep safari type of deal, so you

will be guided around, like a safari, and you will spot the various wildlife as you go. The park is open every day, all year around, and from 6am – 6pm, so you have plenty of scope for visiting.

The park is separated into five different sections, and is home to around 32 different types of mammals, 125 different species of tropical birds, reptiles, flora and fauna, as well as two large rivers which cut the park into two. If you want to spot the wildlife in abundance, then visiting just before the monsoon arrives will give you the best chance.

Udawalawe National Park

If you're an elephant lover, this is the park for you!

This is your chance to get up close and personal with these majestic creatures, and there are also several hotels which are set close to the park too, so you can really focus your attention here. Open from 6am – 6pm again, the park is around 4 hours south of Colombo by car, and again, this is a jeep exploration day out.

Not only will you spot those resident elephants, but you will also be able to see water buffalo, wild boar, jackal, mongooses, spotted deer, foxes, toque macaque, leopard, jungle cats, and many different types of birds too. Stay in the camp for a true wilderness experience!

Wilpattu National Park

This is one of the most scenic national parks by far, with lakes, dense jungle landscapes, and also the home of countless leopards! Because of its beauty, Wilpattu National Park is a little remote, compared to some of the others, and this means that you will probably need to camp and stay over. The park is located around one hour away from Anuradhapura, which is 5 hours away from Colombo by road.

Many people compare this park to the Everglades in Florida, because the wetlands look very similar indeed. This of course means that the range of wildlife, flora and fauna on offer is spectacular, and a jeep safari exploration of this area is a must do. Be on the look out for those leopards, as well as elephants, deer, sloth bear, and plentiful birds.

Minneriya National Park

This is another one for elephant lovers, and it's easy to see large herds together in this particular park – some have seen hundreds together! Located around two hours' drive away from Kandy, this is very accessible park, set within the very scenic centre of the country. You can easily camp here, to give you that wilderness experience, and one of the best times to visit is between May and October, and August and September, as this is when you're likely to see huge numbers of elephants together.

There are of course other animals which call this park home, including 25 different species of reptiles, countless different types of colourful birds, and 24 other species of mammals too.

Bundala National Park

Are you a keen bird-watcher? You can't miss this place then, as this is the number one spot for checking out countless different species of birds on the island. Located in the south-east, the nearest down it Tangalle, on the coast, so you can easily combine beach and wild-life here. The park is a UNESCO protected area, because of the sheer number of different birds which are seen here, including massive groups of flamingos which arrive together during the migration.

It's not all about birds, as many elephants can be spotted here, although a word of warning – due to trouble in the area in the past, the elephants in this region are known to be a little more aggressive than you may find anywhere else; it's simply best to keep a distance and admire them with respect.

Gal Oya National Park

If you want to do something a little different, Gal Oya National Park allows you to take a safari trip by boat! Visit between March to July when there are countless swimming elephants around, and you will be looking at the sight in awe.

Located in the south-east of the island, this park is known for its ecotourism, so you're doing your bit for the environment by visiting. You can also check out countless different types of birds, located in the forest area, check out leopards and elephants in the savanna, and countless types of flora and fauna. Just under half of this park is thick forest, which is a breeding ground for serious nature.

Pinnawala Elephant Orphanage

There are many different elephant sanctuaries and orphanages around the island, but it's best to pick one which is more about the health and safety of the elephants, than it is for giving tourists an elephant ride. This particular orphanage is all about the babies, and it will leave you with tears in your eyes, for sure. You can feed an elephant, learn all about them, and also learn about what the future lies in store for these beautiful baby creatures.

Located around two and a half hours' drive away from Colombo, and one hour away from Kandy.

Nature's Best Attractions & Experiences

Sri Lanka isn't just about animals and wildlife, it's about nature's very best scenery too. Of course, beaches will come into this, but as we mentioned, we're dedicating a full chapter to the wonder of those a little later on. For now, let's focus on the best that Mother Nature has to offer.

Sinharaja Rainforest

This does overlap slightly with the wildlife section, because of course in a rainforest you're going to find wildlife, but this particular rainforest is really jaw-droppingly beautiful in just its appearance.

Trekking & Hiking Opportunities

You might not have Sri Lanka down as a paradise for those who love to get their walking shoes on and indulge in a spot of hiking or trekking, but it really is! There are countless trails for you to try out, and they range from easy, to medium, to high impact options. Wherever you are staying, you're sure to find a trail near you, but there are some which are infamous, and need to be highlighted.

Knuckles Mountains

The central plains are a veritable feast for outdoor adventure fans, and the sights you will see will no doubt stay with you forever. These mountains are around Kandy, so you can easily visit both during your stay. The good thing is that there are trails around here for all ability levels, so there's no excuse not to don those walking boots!

This area covers up to 155 square kilometres and is a combination of different forests, which are home to countless different types of flora and fauna, as well as wildlife too. The trails will all take you through stunning scenery, including across rivers, mountain passes, tea plantations, paddy fields, and basically some of the most beautiful sights you're likely to ever see.

Horton Plains/ World's End/ Baker's Falls

This particular region is where you can truly experience peace and quiet. This region is home to some varied terrain, as well as the famous World's End. This is a plunging cliff which will give you a view to what seems like forever, including the country's most scenic waterfall, Baker's Falls. This waterfall has a viewing platform which you have to visit, to give you a true sense of the power of nature.

The misty hills, the wildlife, the nature, the varied landscapes all make Horton's Plains a definite must trekking experience for anyone who owns a pair of walking boots. There is some altitude involved, but provided you have a good standard of health, you're good to go.

Adam's Peak

Adam's Peak is busiest during December to May, because when the monsoons come, during May to August, this area is difficult to visit. You will need time and a good pair of walking boots to reach it, but the view from the top is divine with a capital D! You'll pass through tea plantations, pass Warana-

gala Falls, water pools, past the Medahinna Temple, and some fantastic places to watch the sunset as you move closer to the summit. As you reach the top, you will see that the terrain gets a little steeper, but it's worth the effort!

Kitulgala & Ella

We will lump these two destinations together, because they are both fantastic outdoor adventure destinations. Kitulgala is fantastic for white water rafting, whether you're a beginner or more advanced, because there is a rapid area for each ability level. This is also where the famous 'Bridge Over The River Kwai' was filmed!

Ella is also a great destination for adrenaline junkies, with climbing, ziplining, and all manner of other activities to enjoy. This is located not too far away from Kandy, and is actually a gap which was formed in the middle of the mountains, dropping down to dense jungle below. Camping here is fantastic, and when you combine it with those outdoor activities to get your blood pumping, you'll have a fantastic experience!

Batatotalena Cave & Belilena Cave (Caving Destinations)

Never tried caving before? Now you can! These are both fascinating natural occurrences, which you can explore with the help of an experienced guide. Batatotalena Cave is near to Sudugala, and once you reach the cave you will be interested to find out more about the archaeological side of things – this cave housed human remnants dating back to 32,000 BC!

Belilena Cave is much easier to visit, because it is close to the resort town of Kitulgala. There is plenty of archaeological importance here too, including the remains of a 12,000 year old civilisation. You can get into the cave via a rope bridge, and explore around to your heart's content.

Under The Sea (And Over it)

The Indian Ocean is a veritable playground for anyone who loves to dive, snorkel, swim, and check out various big sea creatures as they visit the surrounding waters. Basically, if you love what lies beneath, this region is for you! Let's check out what you can do in terms of water-sports, sea animal watching experiences, and diving.

Whale & Dolphin Watching

The waters around the island are packed with things to see and do, but one of the most famous is

without a doubt checking out dolphins and even whales. Some locations only give you a small chance of spotting these majestic creatures, but your chances of seeing them in Sri Lankan waters are thought to be around 95%! You can see blue whales, spinner dolphins, and sperm whales, usually as they are migrating towards Australia and the warmer waters.

There are various locations to be able to spot these beautiful animals, but Mirissa (November to April), Kalpitiya (December to April), and Trincomalee (June to September) are the best spots. There are countless trips from all of these destinations, so you won't struggle to find a tour, either a full day or a half day option.

Diving

Sri Lanka lies within an old trading route, and that means there are many wrecks which can be explored. The oldest shipwreck is thought to be around 2000 years old, and is located near to Hambantota. In addition to this Galle has around 75 wrecks in its waters, and the east coast is also a hotbed of such wrecks too, including HMS Herms, off the cost of Batticaloa, a WW1 aircraft carrier ship.

In the waters around Hikkaduwa there are many coral gardens to explore, as well as glass bottomed boats if you prefer not to get into the water. The marine life around here is

colourful and obscure, in fact Sri Lanka is home to marlin, Spanish mackerel, Benito, Queen Fish barracuda, Grouper, Cobia, Tuna, sail Fish, and Wahoo, to name just a few, as well as turtles too!

Trincomalee is home to deepwater natural harbour, and there are several wrecks around here to explore, snorkelling, and diving opportunities.

Additionally, Kalpitiya Bar Reef Sanctuary is a fantastic place to visit for deep water snorkelling, with a glittering coral reef system to explore. There are around 156 different species of coral and hundreds of different types of marine life in this region, and it is actually home to more biodiversity than you will find anywhere else in the Indian Ocean – that alone should make you want to visit!

You don't have to be a super-experienced diver to enjoy what lies beneath in this particular region either, as standing in water as shallow as two metres will show you brightly coloured fish!

Surfing

Sri Lanka is a great place for experienced surfers, however you should bear in mind that dangerous rip tides can occur at any time, so if you're not so experienced, stick to the shallows. Hikkaduwe is considered to be the best spot for surfing, and this is located on the south-west coast, as well as Arugam Bay, on the east coast. This is actually a good place to learn too, as there is an experienced surf school. Experts say the best time to head here is between May to September, to get the best conditions.

Kitesurfing

Kalpitiya is one of the top

locations for kite surfing, and if you've never tried this aquatic sports, now is the time! You can hire your gear at the kite surfing school, and learn, before trying your luck on the open water.

Deep Sea Fishing

Hikkaduwa is also a fantastic spot for deep sea fishing, and between December to April you will be able to jump on a charter trip and head out into the

open water to see what you can catch! This is also a great way to explore the waters and see the island from a different standpoint.

Cultural Activities

We can't deny the fact that Sri Lanka is a spiritual and cultural place, and if you don't explore that part of the island, you've totally missed the point. The Cultural Triangle, encompassing the wonder of Kandy in particular, is without a doubt the highlight, and if you visit Sri Lanka without going here, you should book yourself a return ticket immediately!

The Cultural Triangle

The northern plains of Sri Lanka are dotted with ancient kingdoms of old and misty hillside villages to explore. The central mountains into that region are therefore dubbed the Cultural Triangle, because in a triangle shape (as the name would suggest) you will find a range of ancient and spiritual landmarks. This is the heartland of Sri Lanka, it's cultural centre.

The area is mainly about Buddhism and the serenity of the natural landscapes really brings that to the fore. You will find countless hillside Buddhist temples, statues of Buddha, sculptures, monasteries which date back thousands of years, and old rock formations which have been changed over the years to be dedicated to Buddhism. When you add in the natural landscapes and soaring mountains, this region is a total treat for the eyes and other senses too.

It's important to remember that you should never pose in front of a statue or sculpture of Buddha, and you should never turn your back to such an object either – this is considered the height of ignorance and rudeness. Bear this in mind.

The Cultural Triangle, despite its popularity, is actually a very quiet and peaceful place, so if you're seeking solitary peace, this is the place for you.

Kandy

Without a doubt the heartland of Sri Lanka, Kandy is

a must visit. This is considered to be the beating heart of the country, and this is where you will find the old Royal Palace, as well as the sacred Tooth of Buddha. Kandy is a UNESCO World Heritage Site, and it was also the former capital of the Sri Lankan Kings.

The other highlight is certainly Degaldoruwe Viharaya, which is a stunningly beautiful Buddhist temple. Make sure you visit Panhalgala, which is a rock located just outside of Kandy, and provides one of the most panoramic and jaw-dropping views over Kandy itself.

There is no better display of opulence, spirituality, and nature in the whole country than you will find in Kandy. Words don't do it justice, the only way for you to appreciate it, is it visit it for yourself.

Dambulla Rock Cave Temple

Another UNESCO World Heritage Site in the Cultural Triangle is Dambulla. Just outside of Kandy, and a short distance away, you will find this stunning example of opulence, culture, and religion. This is one of the world's most famous rock complexes and is full of images and sculptures of Buddha, paintings in the rocks, and nods to ancient history, which dates back over 2500 years.

Sigiriya Rock Fortress

A short distance away from Dambulla, still in the Cultural Triangle, you will find Sigiriya Rock Fortress. This dates back to the 5th century AD, and is another UNESCO listed site.

This is a fortress building that is well preserved, with ramparts, and even a moat

which runs around its exterior. If you head up to the top, you can check out the stunning view for miles, but learning about the history of it is something you must do. This fortress was ordered by King Kashyapa and its frescoes on the western side of the rock, which overlooks the beautiful garden fountains is something you have to see.

Polonnaruwa

Moving on, we have Polonnaruwa, another UNESCO site. This dates back to the 12th century and is a palace complex which is built in honour of royalty of the time. The palace is still in good condition and you can explore the ground floor and walls, including the central piece,

the moonstone. This is carved with decorations of animals and flowers, with echoes of the past all around you.

Anuradhapura

A city which has UNESCO status (can you see a theme emerging here), Anuradhapura was founded in 380BC. The city used to be the capital of the country, and was a city sacred to Buddhism, and you will see countless statues and carvings in honour of Buddha himself. If you walk around the city you will find various archaeological findings, but Tissa Wewa is a must visit, which takes you towards a rock carving – this is meant to be a map of the world, as seen from back in the day. Isurumuniya Temple

is found just beyond this, as well as countless other palaces, temples, and monuments to explore within a small space.

Within Anuradhapura you will also find Mihintale. This is just 11km east of the city itself and is often named as the 'cradle of Buddhism'. It is said that 2350 years ago, Arahath Mahinda Thero, a disciple of Buddha, conveyed the Buddhist religion to royalty at the time.

To reach the actual point, you need to walk up a gruelling 1840 steps, and from there you can see the amazing views, but also the huge Buddha statue. Around here you will also find many caves, which it is thought were the original homes of Buddhist priests

and monks at the time.

Ritigala

To combine nature and history, Ritigala is the place to go. Located high in the mountains, right in the middle of the jungle, inhabited by elephants, leopards, and all manner of other interesting wildlife, this is an important nature reserve which dates back thousands of years, and in fact there is thought to have been inhabitation here from the first century BC, with evidence of several ruins to explore, taking you on a fascinating journey through early history.

Tea Estates in Sri Lanka

Tea and Sri Lanka go hand in hand, so visiting a tea plantation is something that everyone can do. The history of tea in the region goes way back, in fact right back to 1866, when the first estate in Galaha was established. There are several tea plantations and estates throughout the country, but the main ones are Hatton, Dickoya, Nuwara Eliya, and Haputale.

Hatton is really where the heart of tea is found, high in the hills, with sprawling greenery on every side. This is where 'Ceylon Tea' was founded, and you can grab a cup of the special stuff whilst you're there!

Protective Forts Around Sri Lanka

In the northern portion of the country there are countless old forts, ruins of such, which were originally built to protect the country from attempts to invade from various directions. Some have Dutch history, some have British history, and some have Portuguese history, but they are all very impressive. Fort Fredrick, Fort Calpenteyn, Fort Jaffna, and Fort Star are all very well preserved, and can easily be seen during walking expeditions in and around the area. If you're a keen historian, this is a good spot for you to check out.

Galle Fort is one of the easiest to visit, literally in Galle, and it is also one of the most well preserved too. This is a Dutch fort which has UNESCO status, and it is very colourful too. Check out the Old Gate, the Old Dutch Hospital, the Clock Tower, and the impressive views that can be seen from all directions.

These are the main attractions and experiences to have in Sri Lanka during your visit, and it's worth mentioning that these are dotted all over the country. Obviously, if you're only on a short vacation, you need to pick the ones that are closest, but it's also important to check out the thriving city of Colombo too. Let's check out what there is to see and do in the first city you will set eyes on when you arrive on Sri Lankan soil.

Vedda's Indigenous Communities

Vedda is one of the most natural areas in the country, but it is also one of the most cultural, because here you will find indigenous communities, who live in the open air, following totally authentic ways of life. You can do a tour of this area, with the help of a guide, who can help you understand what is going on. Of course, the surroundings are enough to make your jaw drop too, with waterfalls, rainforests, and nearby tea plantations, all set within the dramatic mountains.

What to do in Colombo

Colombo is a big city, and much of its modern-day feel stands in stark contrast to the rest of the country, with its laid-back, serene vibe. This is a good thing though, because if you want a change, a couple of days in the city is ideal! You could either choose to spend some time in Colombo before you leave and head to your resort, being close to the airport already, you could do it at the end of your vacation, or you could easily jump on a bus or a train and head there during your vacation, to split up your time a little.

This being a big city,

there are countless shopping, nightlife, entertainment options to enjoy, but what else is special about this place?

This is a port city, and it is full of colonial history to explore, as well as being close to some fantastic golf courses. All of this overlooks that glittering Indian Ocean too. Be sure to check out the following things when you're in the city:

- Royal Colombo Golf Club – If you love golf, this place is for you
- The open top city tour bus – Yes, it's touristy, but it will show you a lot, in a very short space of time
- Shop 'til you drop – There are several large malls, as well as markets, so you can grab some bargains and souvenirs before you venture home
- Spend time in a top class spa – Colombo has several classy spas to enjoy, and you can really enjoy some relaxing 'me' time, before you head off and perhaps explore a rainforest!
- Gangarama Vihara Temple – You can learn all about Buddhist art here, as there is a museum which will help enlighten you a little, as well as being able to gaze upon the gold opulence of the temple itself
- Dehiwala Zoological Garden – Escape the hustle and bustle for a couple of hours by visiting Dehiwala Zoological Garden. This is packed with wildlife and nature, and covers a huge 30 acres
- Leisure World – If you're visiting with kids, or you're a big kid yourself, check out Leisure World. This is an amusement park which has rides and fun for everyone
- Learn about history at the National Museum of Colombo – Learning about the area is a must do, and it is easy to do here.

These are the top activities to enjoy in Colombo.

Day Trip Options in Sri Lanka

We've talked about the various places to go and what to do, but you can do this from the comfort of an organised tour. There are countless companies who put together these excursions, and it's really a case of finding a company with an itinerary that suits you. Of course, you should always check out the credentials of the company before you part with any cash, and that means checking reviews, the company's listings, any awards they have won, accreditations, insurance, the actual itinerary, as well as the information on guides. Once you're satisfied, you can go ahead!

Some of the most popular day trip excursions, and overnight ones too, include:

- Sightseeing day trips of Colombo – These can either by walking or bus, and will show you the main highlights in one full and fulfilling day.
- Tuk-Tuk trips around Colombo – These are typically with a local English-speaking guide.
- Elephant orphanage tours – This is to Pinnawale, and usually from Colombo. Again, you will have the help of a guide, and you can even bottle feed a baby elephant!
- Sigiriya and Dambulla tour from Colombo – You get to explore to UNESCO sites in one day here, again, with the help of a guide. This is a long and tiring day, but it's one which is more than worth it.
- Sigiriya Rock Fortress and cave temple tour from Kandy – If you're basing yourself in Kandy, you will quickly see that there is plenty to explore, and that knowing about the history of the place is imperative. If you have a

guide to help you out then it becomes infinitely easier, so this tour gives you that benefit, as well as being able to check out two more UNESCO sites, in the heart of Sri Lanka's spiritual lands.

- Nuawara Eliya, Horton Plains and Tea Tours – Again, we're talking about the central and northern plains of the country, and this is where the dramatic landscapes are. You can check out two totally natural, beautiful areas, World's End, Baker's Falls, and you can check out a tea plantation too. If you love tea, this is a must visit!
- Full day checking out Galle and sightseeing – Again, we're talking history here and you have to know the importance of what you're seeing! You can check out Galle Forte, Kottawa pool, the rainforest, and the town itself. This is a busy tourist part of country, and knowing all about it will enrich your visit beyond measure, compared to those who didn't bother to do their homework!
- Sunset at Adam's Peak – Adams Peak (Sri Pada) is beautiful and of course, a sacred part of the country, but at sunset? Totally breath-taking. This is something you can do via a tour, and again, you get a guide to tell you more about its importance.
- Full day tours of Kandy – There is so much to see in Kandy, but if you are on a short time span, it's a good idea to do a tour such as this, because it means you get to see the major highlights, without perhaps wasting your time on parts of the area that don't call out to your particular interests. Again, you get a guide, and that cuts down on time trying to figure out the importance of what you're seeing.
- Madu Ganga River safari – Grab your adventurer's hat! This is a very important ecosystem of Sri Lanka, and the waters and surrounding mangrove

forests are vital to the natural stability of the region. A boat tour down the river will show you the passing landscapes, the wildlife, and the nature at every corner.

- Yala Wildlife Safari – Yala National Park is one of the biggest and most popular national parks in the country, and a guided safari will help you see the wildlife that you really want to see! If you go on your own steam, you might not go at the right time, and you might miss everything; if you go with a guided tour, you have every chance of spotting all the species you love!
- Visiting Vedda's indigenous communities - This is where you can learn about the indigenous communities which call Vedda their home. Living in nature and following traditional ways of life, you can learn all about it and have a truly authentic experience.

Do any of these grab your attention?

Now, if all of this chat has made you peckish, if you're feeling hungry in Sri Lanka, what should you eat and drink?

Chapter 5: Feed Your Belly in Sri Lanka

Visiting any location in the world, be it somewhere new or otherwise, is an extremely good opportunity to do one thing – eat!

Traditional foods should be tried, for the sake of trying them, but also because you never know, you might find yourself a new favourite! Chinese food is delicious, Italian food is divine, Thai food is fragrant and lovely, and Sri Lankan food? This is a mixture of all the above and more!

As with its history, the cuisine on the island is influenced by its past invaders, as well as its neighbours, which creates a real melting pot of tastes and flavours.

When in Sri Lanka, whether you're visiting a beach resort, a city, or somewhere a little more rural, tasting something authentic is a rite of passage. Of course, we're talking about drinks too!

Traditional Sri Lankan Food and Drinks

Foods

Kottu Roti – This is the classic street food dish, and you'll find it everywhere, but very commonly in Colombo. Kottu Roti is a stir fry of sorts, and it has roti, which is a bread, which is them mixed together with vegetables which have been shredded very finely, and then meat, soya sauce, a wonderful blend of spices, including garlic and ginger, and then cooked using a flat skillet.

It sounds complicated, but it's actually a very simple and effective dish to try, and very easy to eat on the go. Oh, it's cheap too!

Lamprais – We talked about Sri Lankan cuisine being influenced by the past, and this really sums it up, as it has its origins in Holland. Now, lamprais sounds odd, but bear with us; this is basically boiled eggs, aubergine (egg-plant), beef meat balls (which is the part which originates in Holland), and other meats mixed together. There is a vegetarian option available, as soya will be used, but this is then mixed together with various delicious spices from the area, including cardamom, as well as rice. The mixture is spooned into a banana leaf and then baked. Truly delicious!

Dhal – This is where India influences Sri Lankan food, because this curry dish has links to both countries. Dhal curry is basically lentils, usually the red variety, and they mixed together with delicious and creamy coconut milk. Add in green chillies, tomatoes, and onions, with a few different spices, including mustard seeds, and then cook in the oven. Yummy.

Gotu Kola Mallung – This is a salad dish, which is often served as an accompaniment to many different meals, but can be a healthy option on its own. Packed with vitamins, you could even say this is a superfood in a dish! Mallung is a kale type of leaf, and this is mixed together with other green leaves and chillies, ginger, coconut, and other pieces, to make a delicious salad mixture.

Eggplant Moju (Wambatu) – This dish will vary slightly depending on where you are in the country, as everyone likes to do it differently, but it is basically slices of aubergine (eggplant), which are friend and then chilli powder is added, mustard seeds, sugar, vineyard and cloves, which makes a delicious and tangy sauce. This is then served with rice. Again, it sounds strange, but you have to try it to appreciate its wonderfulness!

Egg Hoppers – Basically this is a pancake with a fried egg in the middle, but there's more to it than meets the eye! Add in onions, chillies, lemon juice and a little salt, as well as a delicious and tangy coconut relish to the mixture, poured over the pancake and egg. This is a general Indonesian dish, but has regional differences on the island.

Fish Ambul Thiyal – This is basically a fish curry which has a slightly sour taste – bear with us! Tuna is usually the fish of choice here, cut into chunks and then cooked with various delicious spices. Dried go-raka, a fruit, is then added to the mixture, to give it that sour taste. All of this is cooked further with a little water, to create a curry, before allowing it to dry out slightly.

Drinks

Wood Apple Juice – Yes, it is what it sounds like, but with a difference! This is another street drink, which you will find everywhere. A wood apple is a fruit, and it is actually a paste which is combined with water and mixed together. It's delicious, you should try it!

Ceylon Tea – No surprises here, but you have to try the traditional stuff whilst you're visiting! We know that Sri Lanka is famous for its tea production, in fact it is the world's third biggest producer. It's worth mentioning that tea in the heart of the country is often very sweet, because locals will add a lot of sugar! This will be added without you having to ask, so if you don't have too much of a sweet tea, mention this at the time of ordering.

King Coconut Juice – The delicious exotic fruits which are grown on the island also produce some delicious juice drinks, and king coconut trees are found everywhere. The juice of this is sweet and has a lot of natural health benefits too; this is often used in traditional Ayurvedic alternative medicines.

Toddy – This is an alcoholic drink, but not particularly strong, and is made from coconut palm sap which has fermented. Is it like beer? Not really, it's actually quite vinegary in taste, but you have to try it.

Arrack – This is another alcoholic drink, but much

stronger than toddy! If you like rum, or you're a keen whisky drinker then you'll probably like this. Arrack is a distilled drink of palm syrup, or even toddy which has gone even more alcoholic. You can mix it with a soft drink, such as lemonade or coke, or you can drink it straight – it depends how much of a kick you're trying to get!

Faluda – If you like milky drinks, you should try faluda. This is made of milk, jelly, and rose syrup, to give a sweet, thick beverage. Try it ice cold for a really refreshing treat.

Elephant House Ginger Beer – This is one of Sri Lanka's most famous exports, and one which you have probably tried outside of the country. This drink actually has natural healing elements, and is made using ginger with Ayurvedic functions. Many people drink it after food, because it is known to help with digestion and avoid indigestion symptoms.

As you can see, Sri Lankan food is certainly spicy and has a burst of flavour no matter what dish you're trying, and it's also the case with the drinks too, which are far from conventional! This is what makes cuisine in this part of the world so delicious – it's different, and a total break from the norm. Whatever you do however, be careful how much arrack you drink, it's potent stuff!

Top Restaurants to Try in Sri Lanka

Of course, we can't mention every restaurant on the island, because we simply don't have enough room or time, but we can give you some top choices that many people have stated as being packed with delicious foods, great service, and more often than not, a fantastic view too. No matter where you are in the country, you won't struggle to find somewhere to fill your belly, whether that is a big, fancy restaurant (usually found in Colombo), or a small family-run joint.

Let's check out a few of the top choices in the main tourism areas on the island

Restaurants in Colombo

The Lagoon – For a special occasion, The Lagoon is where it's at, and it's a fantastic place to try fresh seafood too. Not the cheapest, but great for a first night, or perhaps when you want to splash the cash for something a little different, the ocean sushi is thought to be the best in the area, as well as the shoe lobster. A definite for seafood fans!

Paradise Road, The Gallery Café – It sounds opulent, and it is, but the surroundings are quite rustic, which helps you relax, despite the price tag! Another for seafood lovers, but with a large menu of international dishes too, the black pork is a signature dish, with some delicious desserts to check out too – try the caramel cheesecake!

Tasty Caterers – You might not want to spend a fortune whilst you're in Colombo, and the good news is that there are many budget options too, including Tasty Caterers. The pastries are said to be fantastic here, but the lasagne is always a favourite too! A great option for those who want comfort food with lower price tags, and those who always want a large international menu to try.

Momo's by Ruvi – This family run establishment is cosy and fun, and it isn't as expensive as it might sound either! This is a great place for traditional foods from the whole Asian area, and the dumplings are some of the best you'll find on the whole island!

The London Grill – Taking its name from its former history, The London Grill will give you plentiful international options, and the steak is always very highly recommended. Another restaurant which is mid-priced, but which also has a fun and laid-back atmosphere. Great for families or couples in particular.

Restaurants in Jaffna

Mangos – This is a very highly rated restaurant for anyone looking for traditional cuisine. Check out the masala dosa, which is always mentioned as a top choice. The price isn't high, and the atmosphere is also as laid-back as the area you're visiting. This is a good choice for families.

Jetwing Jaffna – For those wanting something a little more sophisticated, it has to be Jetwing Jaffna. Very highly rated, but also with a slightly higher price tag, this restaurant serves all the international alcoholic drink brands, as well as offering local and international dishes. The breakfast buffet is also a great way to start your day.

Akshathai – It sounds traditional, and it is! This is a great way to try some of those dishes we were talking about in our last section, with many different curries on the menu too. If you love an Indian meal, with a Sri Lankan twist thrown in for good measure, you're sure to enjoy your evening here.

Vishnu Bavan – This is a restaurant that caters very well for vegetarians, which isn't always the case in a country which is so meat heavy. Again, the dosa dishes are renowned, and the price tag isn't high either. Try the ghee dhosai, which always get a special mention.

Malayan Café – Located in the Grand Bazaar area, you'll get a really authentic experience by visiting this restaurant. The interior looks basic but the food is far from it, with a large range of different curries on offer.

Restaurants in Kandy

Licensed to Grill – The name is great, and the food is too! As the name would suggest, this is a barbeque restaurant, which serves all manner of delicious meaty dishes, as well as some international options too. The burgers are quite famous around here! If you're visiting as a family and you have children in tow, this is a great option.

Balaji Dosai – Another restaurant which is for the vegetarians amongst you, the dishes are traditional and meat-free, which means you can relax and not have to worry about finding something on the menu. On a side note, the coffee here is said to be some of the best around the area.

Buono – A great place to try local dishes, but also for those who want the safety net of international dishes too. The inside of the restaurant looks just like a family kitchen, which gives it a charming feel. Try the donuts and cakes in particular, the restaurant is renowned for its desserts!

The Kandy Garden Café – For a quick snack on the go, this is a great option, in really laid back surroundings. Great for families, but also those who just want something quick and easy, you can enjoy curries and burgers in the same sitting!

Citrus Café and Restaurant – The egg roti and curries in this restaurant are the particular favourites, and the surroundings are classy yet laid back too. Perfect for those who want to have a slightly more upmarket meal, but who don't want to spend a fortune at the same time.

Restaurants in Arugam Bay, Trincomalee, & Nilaveli

Tandoori Hut, Arugam Bay – The outside of the restaurant looks like it is hidden away, but once you're inside, you're literally sat inside the gardens! This makes for a wonderful difference, and the food is also very highly recommended. Try the tandoori chicken and vindaloo, for mainstream dishes with a slight twist.

Mr Fisherman, Arugam Bay – The name suggests this is a seafood restaurant, and that is what it is! Despite that, don't expect huge price tags, which is what really pulls in visitors, as well as the simple exterior, with charming fairy lights hanging from the trees. The lobster is particularly highly rated.

Trinco Lanka Restaurant, Trincomalee – This restaurant almost looks like a surf shack, but that's the laid back charm! You can choose from sea food, curries, and even upmarket lobster, all within a charming atmosphere. This restaurant is renowned for its friendly and fast service. A great way to spend a full day!

Gaga Restaurant, Trincomalee – If you love seafood, but you don't want to spend a fortune, this is a great option. The meals are very large, so you'll need to be hungry to eat here! Try the red snapper or the cuttlefish, for something a little different.

Siva Restaurant, Nilaveli – This restaurant is like a home away from home, with some seriously delicious local dishes to try, in friendly surroundings. Check out the chicken curry, which is much more tasty than you might think, as well as the rotis, and the seafood on offer. This is a BBQ restaurant, so there is a large range of meaty dishes on offer.

Restaurants in Kalpitiya, Marawila & Waikkal

Dolphin Beach Resort Restaurant, Kalpitiya – This isn't the cheapest option, but it's certainly one for anyone who wants something different, or to celebrate a special occasion. The seafood is amazing, the atmosphere is laid back, and almost romantic, and the menu is made of food with totally fresh, local ingredients.

Café Wave, Kalpitiya – Located in pretty beach huts, this restaurant is a great laid back option, and one which will suit families and couples alike. The prawns are said to be great here, as well as the delicious salads and the exotic fruit juices, freshly squeezed.

O2 Seafood Restaurant, Marawila – One word – lobster! For those who love cheap but delicious seafood, this is the place for you! Located right on the seafront, you can admire the view whilst trying all manner of delicious fishy dishes – try the seafood platter for a bit of everything.

Sunny Restaurant, Waikkal – Sunny by name, and sunny by nature, this restaurant is charming and bright, and offers a range of dishes from the Asian area. Again, seafood is

prominent, but the curries are also very highly recommended too.

Prego, Waikkal – Are you craving some international food? Do you love Italian? This is the place to go! This Italian restaurant, far, far away from Italy itself, serves some delicious pasta, pizza dishes, and will fill your cravings until you go home.

Restaurants in Nuwara Eliya & Bandarawela

Grand Indian, Nuwara Eliya – For curries in the Nuwara Eliya region, this is where you need to be going. Prices are mid-range, and the restaurant is like a house conservatory, making you feel at home. Try the butter chicken and the naan bread for a delicious comfort food meal, or the black daal in particular.

Barnes Hall, Nuwara Eliya – This is a seriously classy affair, so if you're trying to find somewhere a little more sophisticated than a surf shack, this is for you. A little more pricey, but worth it for the experience, be sure to try the buffet breakfast, which is by far the most packed and traditional in the whole area.

Grand Thai, Nuwara Eliya – Traditional Thai restaurant are often quite opulently decorated, and this particular choice is no different. From soups to noodles, seafood to curries, the menu is large, and you're sure to find something to tickle your taste buds.

Matey Hut, Bandarawela – If you're tired after a full day exploring nearby Ella, then Matey Hut is the place to go. As friendly as it sounds, the curries here are said to be the best in the area, and the prices are low too.

Ceylon Tea Factory Restaurant, Bandarawela – Yes, it says it's a tea factory, but it's actually a very delicious local restaurant. Try the baked crab or the prawn curry for a real seafood taste hit, and of course, a cup of tea has to be included too!

Hopefully, this particular section will have had you feeling hungry at the very start, and ravenous by this point! When in Sri Lanka, no matter where you are basing yourself, be sure to head to a couple of these choices, for some of the best meals around.

Of course, you're sure to find countless bars too, particularly in the Colombo area, and in the tourist regions. Hotels tend to have one or more choices on-site, which will cater for your evening's entertainment.

Now, where to stay?

Chapter 6: Where to Stay in Sri Lanka

Obviously, you're going to need somewhere to lay your head when you visit Sri Lanka, and happily, there are all manner of different options available to you. For instance, if you want to splash the cash, there are some seriously swanky hotels you can opt for, meaning that you totally get to chill the hell out in blissful surroundings; on the other hand, there are more budget options too, as

well as campsites and hostels. As you can see, Sri Lanka is a destination for everyone, no matter what the budget.

You probably didn't even think that when you first thought about the idea of visiting, right? Well, most destinations have their surprises, and accommodation in Sri Lanka can be much cheaper than you think.

It's not as easy to organise hotels as it is restaurants, so this particular section is going to give you an overview of some of the best hotels and hostels on the island as a whole. This means that you can pick somewhere suiting your price range, as we are going to organise them from cheapest first, up to the most expensive. Bear in mind that we can't give specific prices, because they are going to fluctuate, and we don't want to give you false information, but if you work from the top downwards, you get an idea of how much cash you're likely to need for booking.

Obviously, city hotels are going to be a little more per night than the resorts, so if you're wanting to say in Colombo, expect to pay a fraction more than you might pay when you visit a beach resort, or another smaller town.

Budget Priced Accommodation

Backpack Lanka, Colombo – Hostels are not what they used to be, and nowadays they are more like budget hotels. This two star option is right in the heart of Colombo, and gives visitors the ideal base for exploring further. Guests will have a hearty breakfast included in the price, and rooms are basic but comfortable, with 26 rooms available, and a communal kitchen if you need a snack of an evening; despite that, there is a restaurant on-site too.

Ceylonica Beach Hotel, Negombo – Located on a beautiful stretch of beach, surrounding by palm trees, and in the ideal spot for sunset lovers, Ceylonica Beach Hotel offers guests a budget choice, in amazing surrounding. The bed and breakfast choice means you can fuel up during the day, and the hotel is located just 5 minutes away from Negombo Beach Park. All rooms are also thankfully air conditioned, and there is an on-site restaurant for your meals.

Kandyan View Holiday Bungalow, Heerassagala – This hotel has a real home away from home feel, with a bed and breakfast option. The hotel is right on top of a hill, with sweeping views over Kandy itself, and the mountains in the distance. Rooms have flat screen TVs and tea and coffee making facilities, giving you a really comfortable base for your exploration of this beautiful area of the country.

Sai Sea City Hotel, Colombo – This is another small and quiet hotel, which is also very handily based just outside the centre of the city. Rooms come with a bed and breakfast or room only option, and you can opt to pay a little more for a sea view, if you wish. There are only 30 rooms on-site, so it is never crowded or busy, and there are two restaurants on-site, as well as a coffee shop and room service facilities.

Milano Tourist Rest, Anuradhapura – Located in the centre of the historical town, this hotel offers you a really comfortable place to relax and rest, in some beautiful surroundings. The rooms all have TVs and air conditioning, with a room only basis for booking. There are two restaurants on-site, one indoors and one outdoors, and a bar on the roof terrace – all for a surprisingly low price.

Mid Priced Accommodation

Ranveli Beach Resort, Dehiwala – This hotel is impressive, and despite it being a tad more expensive than our other choices, it is still cheap for what you will be getting. The hotel comes with a bed and breakfast option, and is located centrally, so you can easily get out and about without any trouble. There are 32 rooms in the hotel, which are all air-conditioned, as well as double and family rooms too. Rooms also mostly have a balcony, so you can chill out at the end of the day.

The Saffron, Colombo – Located in the centre of the city, this hotel is small but charming, with just 12 rooms on-site. This is a very popular hotel with return guests, so it's a good idea to book ahead of time. The rooms all overlook the landscaped gardens, and there is room service and high quality Wi-Fi for guests to enjoy. This is a great base for your city exploration.

Time N Tide Beach Resort, Hikkaduwa – If you want to stay literally right on the beach, this is for you! This bed and breakfast establishment is a great place to stay, and one which is also very popular. There are 17 rooms on-site, so you're never going to feel like you're in the middle of a busy resort base, and you will find many amenities there too, including an on-site restaurant with international menus, as well as an excursion desk, so you can find out about exploring the area much easier.

Clarion Hotel, Kiribathgoda – This hotel looks seriously impressive from the outside, and it's actually a cheaper choice than it looks. This is a room only basis, and it is located in Kiribathgoda, which means you can easily get to Colombo, without being in the middle of it all. There is an on-site fitness centre, steam room, and salon, and you can choose from standard, superior, or deluxe type rooms.

Hotel Elephant Park, Pinnawala – Elephant lovers rejoice! This is your chance to stay literally minutes away from the famous elephant orphanage, located right in the heart of the natural habitat Sri Lanka is so famous for. There are just 7 rooms on-site, so it's super quiet and peaceful, and there is also an on-site restaurant and bar too. If you want to upgrade to a room with a balcony, you may even be able to spot the majestic creatures in the distance.

High End Accommodation

Saman Villas, Bentota – Think about infinity pools, amazing beach views, luxury, and amazing service, and you've basically got Saman Villas in your mind! The superior suites, deluxe suites, and double standard room options mean that there is a choice for everyone, and you can go for the bed and breakfast basis, or a half board, depending on your preference. The hotel is decorated in traditional Sri Lankan temple style and really gives you an exclusive experience.

Reef Villa & Spa, Wadduwa – Choose from three different suite types, including the Ocean Suite with sweeping and stunning views, and this is a hotel that will be truly once in a lifetime. The basis is room only, and the on-site bar and restaurant is there to cater for your needs. As the name would suggest, there is also a spa on-site, so you can enjoy treatment, as well as massages, and the indoor and outdoor pools. Total bliss!

Anantara Peace Haven Tangalle Resort, Tangalla – If you want to give yourself a truly memorable experience here, pick the Premier Ocean View Room – yes, it is expensive, but it's amazing too! Rooms are large, sleeping up to three adults, or two adults and a child, with still plentiful room to roam about. You can also choose from bed and breakfast, half board, or full board, and the on-site facilities will have you wanting to stay, including the spa, pool, views, and the coconut grove which surrounds the hotel.

Siddhalepa Ayurveda Health Resort, Wadduwa – Sri Lanka is well known for its Ayurveda medicine, and this particular resort is aimed towards helping you unwind, de-stress, and basically focus your mind and energy back into somewhere positive and helpful to you. Of course, it doesn't hurt that the hotel is also set right on the beach and in lush green rainforest either! This is a full board hotel, which offers you rooms with a private spa tub and flat screen TV. Basically, you will want for nothing.

Jetwing Saint Andrews, Nuwara Eliya – If you want to feel like you are royalty, staying in an old Sri Lankan palace, then this is a great go-to. The hotel is surrounded by forests and vegetation, with lakes and nearby restaurants to enjoy. You're not totally cut off from the world however, as there are buses which run by the hotel grounds, taking you into the town. Rooms are large, opulent, and very spacious, with the bed and breakfast option fuelling you up for the day.

Campsites & Wilderness Stays

Of course, the natural landscapes of Sri Lanka mean that camping and staying out in the wilderness is a must do, if you can. You don't have to base your entire vacation in this type of place, but you can dib in and out of it, almost like a safari break, if you will. There are countless campsites which will cater for your needs, some basic, some in the middle, and some which are seriously sophisticated and luxurious – ever wanted to go glamping?

Let's check out five of the best campsites you might like to consider as part of your vacation.

Pardus Seek Luxury Camping, Palatupana – Located close to Leopard Rock and Palatupana Beach, this is camping with a luxurious twist; forget about tents, and think more along the lines of your own wooden bungalow instead. There are even en-suite bathrooms! You can head off on a wildlife safari, you can enjoy luxury dining in the on-site restaurant, and this is all in the middle of the jungle!

Yala Safari Camping, Yala National Park – Yala National Park is one of the most famous in Sri Lanka, and the fact that you can enjoy camping in the wilderness, whilst being waited on hand and foot is really special! 'Rooms' consist of large wooden bungalows with open sides to give you the air you need during those warm nights, and you can enjoy BBQ food and drinks every single day.

Tree Tops Jungle Lodge, Buttala – If you love elephants, birds, and general wildlife, then a break in this beautiful space will be just up your street! Tents are not the traditional types, they are wooden shacks which give you a much more comfortable place to stay during your wilderness break. The on-site restaurant will also fill your catering needs, and there are plentiful safari options to take you out and about too.

As you can see, there are a variety of options available to you, no matter what you choose to do with your time on the island. There are also countless more accommodation options, but we simply don't have the paper or time to write about them all! This selection certainly shows you the type of quality and range you can expect, so you can take your search from there and tailor-make it to your requirements.

Let's Go to The Beach!

Have we saved the best bit until almost last? Probably so! Sri Lanka's beaches are legendary, beautiful, and they are places that will wash away every single one of your cares, right out into the middle of the vast Indian Ocean. Put simply, it's impossible to be worried, upset, depressed anxious, or any other kind of negative connotation, when you are faced with aquatic beauty such as this.

Of course, this being an island, there are miles and miles of coastline, but that doesn't mean that every spot of sand is as quality as another! For that reason, you need to know the best spots to go, in order to really get that castaway Sri Lankan vibe that you've probably been dreaming of. If you really want to set your imagination on fire, just Google Sri Lanka beaches, and see what dreamy images come to your mind!

We know that Sri Lanka has the glittering Indian Ocean on every single side of it, and that means plentiful diving spots. We mentioned these in our section on things to see and do, but it's worth highlighting that many spots will mean you can simply paddle out to the shallows and check out marine-life, you don't need to be an expert swimmer, or an expert diver to be able to check out some of the underwater residents of this beautiful region of the world. That being said, do be aware that riptides can sometimes arise out of nowhere from time to time, and that you should always heed advice from coastguards. If there is a flag there, warning you not to pass that point, then under no circumstances should you pass that point!

If you're travelling with children, there are some beaches which are safer than others, and you should always keep an eye on little ones playing in and near the water.

Okay, warning out of the way, let's check out some of the best beaches on the island. It's definitely worthwhile visiting several, as they are all subtly different in their beauty and make-up.

Hikkaduwa Beach

This is a resort part of the island, so you can expect plentiful tourism facilities, which will make your break much easier, especially if you're travelling as a family, but it is still peaceful and chilled out regardless. You can check out many different diving and snorkelling spots just off the

shore, or you can simply kick back and relax – the choice is yours!

The town literally runs down to the beach itself, so you can head off and have a break if you want to find, a small café or surf shack for a drink perhaps, before venturing back to the sand. It's worth mentioning that seafood around this particular beach is fantastic, so for seafood fans, this is a must visit!

Be warned that during November to April and January to March, you can expect larger crowds here, but it is never totally packed either way.

Unawatuna Beach

Again, we're talking about a tourist resort area, so plentiful hotels and

restaurants are around this beach. Nearby Galle means you can do town and beach time together, and this is also a good beach for families, because the waters are a little calmer than some other beaches around the island, especially in April and November.

This is a wide sweeping arch of a beach, with crystal clear waters. It can get a little busy, because it is very popular with locals, and because of its close proximity to Colombo and Galle, that means that weekend visitors are quite happy to venture out for the day at any time.

Nilaveli Beach

Total rest and relaxation is not difficult to find on Nilaveli Beach because, here more than anywhere else, the water seems bluer and the sand seems whiter. Just a short distance away from Trin-

comalee, this beach is much quieter than some of the other options around, so you can really kick back and relax during your day on the sand.

You can take a boat ride to nearby Pigeon Island, which has a coral reef to explore, and that will really make you feel like you're miles away from anyone and everything! Between May to September is thought to be the best time to visit this beach, to avoid the monsoon season, and this is also when visitors are likely to be more so, yet still never enough to be crowded.

Passekudah Bay

On the eastern coastline you will find the beauty of Passedukah Bay. This area is just outside of Batticaloa, and is great for paddling and sunbathing, in its relatively quiet surroundings. This is a quieter beach again, a real

hidden gem in many ways, and will never be crowded. Swimming here is thought to be safe, provided you heed advice regarding flags and from the coast-guard, and that is because there is a reef which is just off the coast, protecting the area from the larger waves.

September is a great time to visit this particular area, when the weather is beautiful, and surfing at nearby Kalkudah Beach is a real sight to see.

Arugam Bay Beach

This particular beach is the place to go if you love surfing, but only if you're experienced! Of course, if you're not a keen surfer, that doesn't mean you can go and watch, whilst soaking up the sun. From April to October you will see the best surfing conditions, which also means the largest waves – always be careful!

Because of the surfer vibe around this region,

that means that it is very laid back, very chilled, and ideal for anyone who simply want a slow pace of life, without much else going on.

Negombo Beach

This beach can get busy, because it is only around an hour from Colombo, which draws locals and visitors alike. The sunsets here are legendary, and there is a lively atmosphere all around, with music, bars, restaurants, and all manner of chilled out fun to be had.

This is a great idea for

families, because there is so much going on, but also for groups looking for fun too.

Kalpitiya Beach

This is basically where most people go to jump on a whale watching expedition, but the beach is certainly worth an exploration too!

The whale watching season is best experienced between February to March, when there are sperm whales and spinner dolphins around, but November to April is when the waters are at their

calmest, and therefore best for swimming and family fun.

Tangalle Beach

This particular beach is considered to be a real hidden gem, with a few other rocky and sheltered bays just around the corner. The best time to visit this beach is April to October, when the best of the weather is present, and less in the way of rain. There is also likely to be much less crowded conditions regardless, and that means you can really grab a drink and relax, in a true Castaway style!

Bentota Beach

If you love water-sports then Bentota Beach is a great spot for you. Deep sea fishing is particularly good around this part of the coast, but there is also the chance to wind surf, water ski, snorkel, scuba dive, swim, and canoe. Basically, the waters here are safer, especially during November to April, so you can rest assured that you're going to be protected.

The downside is that it can get crowded during this time too, because this is a renowned beach for water-sports and aquatic fun!

This is by no means an exhaustive list, because with an island's entire coastline to explore, it's not possible to mention all the top spots. The main ones are here however, including the best times to venture there and enjoy the weather and safe water conditions.

We have to stress again – riptides can be dangerous and unpredictable at times outside of these recommended ones, so never venture out unaided, or basically at all, outside of these times. The Indian Ocean may be stunning-

ly beautiful, but it has claimed many a ship over the years, due to its tumulus nature, and because of the varied weather conditions that come and go unpredictably over the course of the calendar year, it's important to heed advice. Mother Nature is unforgiving sometimes, especially when you don't listen to her!

It's definitely worthwhile combining your Sri Lankan beach time with a city break and some cultural time too. There are some destinations which cater purely for beach time, and that's fine, but an island as enriching as this is about so much more. If you don't get out and explore, if you don't mix it up and enjoy a bit of everything, then you're not really 'getting' the true heart of Sri Lanka at all.

You need your walking boots, your city gear, and your swimming costume/ trunks all in the same suitcase for this type of vacation, whether you're staying in one place or exploring a few!

Chapter 8: Health and Safety in Sri Lanka

As with any country in the world, there are certain things you need to know, in order to keep you safe and healthy during your travels. Some of these things are really common sense, i.e. don't leave your brain at the airport when you depart, but some of them are a little more in-depth, and pertinent to the country itself.

This chapter is going to tell you everything you need to know about staying healthy and safe when visiting Sri Lanka. You might roll your eyes at some of our suggestions, because as we mentioned just now, it's common sense, but many people, all of us included, have a habit of letting our guards down a little too much when we jet off somewhere new. How many times have you seen someone riding on the back of a motorcycle with no helmet on when on vacation? Yet, when that person is at home, they are the most straight-laced, sensible person around? This is a case of brain left at airport syndrome, and something we should all be trying to avoid! Of course, there's nothing to say you can't have fun, in fact fun it up to the max, but safety should always come first.

Let's explore both health and safety in two different sections.

Health Issues

The advice for health issues related to Sri Lanka

is pretty much the same as most other destinations in the region.

- Make sure all your immunisations are up to date before you head away, and have a health check with your healthcare professional if you have any concerns before flying.
- Visit your healthcare professional around 4-6 weeks before you travel, to check whether you need any additional vaccinations or other treatments for prevention of disease. This changes regularly, and it often depends on the region you're travelling to, so get advice from the people in the know.
- There is a risk from mosquitoes across the whole country, so make sure you take steps to prevent bites. Dengue Fever is known to be caused by a mosquito bite, and there

have been many cases over the last year.

- Always make sure you have adequate travel and health insurance which will cover you for any hospital treatment in an emergency.
- Hospitals in Sri Lanka are good, but they are probably not to the standard you would experience back home, especially if you travel away from the main city of Colombo. If you venture to a private hospital then you can expect to pay more for your treatment, so again, good quality insurance is key.
- Always wear high SPF sun-cream, stay out of the sun during the peak afternoon hours, wear a hat, and always drink plenty of bottled water. Sun safety is key, whether it is monsoon season or not.
- Be wary of alcoholic measures overseas, no matter where you're travelling, as these may be stronger than you are used to. On top of this, never leave your drink unattended, and never accept a drink from anyone you don't know – drink spiking is known in Sri Lanka.
- Always drink bottled water, and never from the tap. Be wary of ice which is made with tap water, and any salads which have been washed with tap water also.
- If you experience the famous upset stomach, e.g. diarrhoea, vomiting, or both, make sure you drink plenty of water and stay indoors where it is cool. This should pass quite quickly, but if it doesn't seek medical attention.

As you can see, all pretty standard advice, but it pays to be aware!

Safety Issues:

Terrorism

Unfortunately, we live in a world where we are practically at war with most people over something, and one of the most terrifying things which is present on our planet is terrorism. We have to mentioned it, as scary as it is, because it is so pertinent these days. Sri Lanka isn't known for terrorism per se, but it can't be ruled out. For that reason, you should always listen to travel advice, keep an eye on the news, and basically do whatever is advised of you by the people you should trust – by this, we are talking about the consulate website of your particular country of origin. For instance, if (God forbid) something happens whilst you're away, and your consulate is telling your nationals to leave, then you should leave. Of course, this is very unlikely to happen, but to highlight a point.

Sri Lanka has a rather tumulus past, with a civil war raged between the Government and the Tamil Tigers (Liberation Tigers of Tamil Eelam). This thankfully came to an end in 2009, but that doesn't mean that the occasional flashpoint can't occur from time to time. Basically, the advice in this regard is to avoid visiting any areas which are known to be mainly military, e.g. bases. These parts of the country have no interest to tourism anyway, so simply stay away. On top of this, avoid any gatherings which are political rallies, etc.

The northern part of the country used to be a no-go zone, because this was the part of the country where conflict was mainly ongoing, but now this is not the case. You can now visit the northern portion of the country openly, however do be aware that there is the slight risk of unexploded landmines, which are currently being recovered by the army. Another area which is highlighted in terms of landmines is Jaffna Peninsula's Elephant Pass. Again, be vigilant, as well as in the Kilinochchi, Mullaittivu, Mannar, and Vavuniya areas. The east of the country is also a slight risk in this regard, so simply pay attention and look for any possible landmine warning signs.

If you are stopped by a member of the military or the police at any time during your stay, you will be asked to show your passport, and for that reason, always keep it with you. If you don't have it, you could land yourself in hot water, and that's not something you want to be remembering from your time away.

Crime

Sri Lanka is just the same as any other country in terms of crime, it happens. That being said, crime against visiting tourists is known to be quite low, but that doesn't mean you shouldn't be vigilant at all times. Never carry a large number of valuable belongings with you, don't flash your new iPhone for all to see, keep the amount of cash on you to a minimum, and keep a copy of your passport in the hotel safe, just in case.

If you are a victim of crime, report this to the police immediately.

One particular issue which is a little more prevalent is credit card fraud. The best advice to avoid this is to use ATMs which are attached to banks or big hotels, and not the hole in the wall that you see randomly on the street. Keep your credit card with you at all times, and never let a restaurant member of staff or a vendor take it away from you, out of your sight.

Advice For Women

Whilst men should always be just as vigilant when

travelling, women should pay extra attention. There have been reports of sexual attacks on tourist women lately, and for that reason, women should always pay extra attention when out and about. Much of this is common sense, don't walk alone, don't trust anyone you haven't met before, don't get into a car you don't recognise, never accept a drink from a stranger, and never leave your drink unattended. Drink spiking is a common tactic employed in this regard. It's always a good idea to keep a small personal alarm in your bag.

Whilst this all sounds rather scary, we do have to put it into perspective. This is very unlikely to happen, but even the smallest chance means that we should be informed and on our guard. The risk in Sri Lanka is actually no higher than any other country the world over, but in the interests of your safety and completeness, let's just mention it.

Swimming and Sea Safety

The Indian Ocean is a beautiful, glittering place, but it does have its perils. The waters around Sri Lanka have been known to be rather dangerous at certain times of the year, when high tides can create high waves and perilous rip tides. If there is a warning flag in place, heed that advice. Swimming against advice is only going to land you in hot water, in more ways than one.

Customs and Respect Issues You Need to Know About

One of the greatest things about visiting Sri Lanka is the vast number of different customs and traditions you'll come into contact with. As this is life and that means there is a downside to every upside, this also means that there is a risk you could come a cropper if you don't know how to traverse this rather confusing situation. Never fear! We're going to help you do just that.

Consider this your guide to surviving custom and respect issues, your 101 to avoiding hot water!

'Handy' Issues

You will notice more often than not in the rural areas of Sri Lanka, that most people eat with their right hands, using the fingertips. You will probably be offered a knife and fork, but locals don't use them. It's a good idea to try and copy the locals, because this will certainly gain you some traveller respect, but it also means you're down with the culture yourself! Messy? A little, but so much easier on the person doing the washing up!

You'll also find that basically everything is done with the right hand, so if you're shaking hands with someone, go right, and if you're giving them sometimes, use your right hand again.

Respect for Buddhism and Buddha

This is probably the most important thing to mention. The mistreatment in any way of a Buddhist picture, image, statue, artefact, or anything related to the religion is serious, and it has been known to carry conviction punishment. On top of this, if you have a tattoo of Buddha, you need to hide it constantly, because this considered hugely disrespectful, and it has been known that travellers have been turned away at the airport and sent back home. Of course, this extends to items of clothing or images on bags or accessories.

It's also forbidden to have photographs taken in front of statues of Buddha, which you will see plentifully. It's okay to take a photograph of the statue itself, but don't be posing in front of it. Everyone should be facing the statue, with nobody turned towards the camera lens. Basically, follow the lead of the locals, and that way you can't go wrong.

This is a case of religious respect, and unless you want to find yourself in trouble, and probably faced with an angry group of people in front of you, be sure to practice the deepest respect for the island's cultures, customs and religions.

Of course, we know that religion is a difficult subject to talk about, and whilst it's perfectly fine to ask questions if you get to know someone, or of a tour guide, you should do this in a very sensitive manner, and you should never try to delve too deep. Inquisitiveness in order to learn is fine, but anything more than that is considered intrusive and rude. It's probably best just to avoid the subject altogether.

If you are visiting a Buddhist temple, always dress modestly and respectfully. Make sure your legs are covered and your shoulders too. If you are wearing a hat, take it off, and always take off your shoes too, before you enter the building. When inside, be quiet, be respectful, and simply soak up the serenity and the atmosphere. Buddhist temples are simply divine in decoration, and visiting one is a definite must do during your time in Sri Lanka.

On a final note, Buddhist monks should be treated with the utmost respect. Never touch them, never touch their head in particular, and always give up your seat on a bus or train.

Photography Issues

Be very careful what you take photographs of. We've covered the issue of statues of Buddha, but this also extends to other areas, such as military areas, Government buildings, and any car or vehicle which is used by Government officials, or important people. Basically, if you see soldiers guarding anything, don't take photographs.

You will see signs which prohibit photography from time to time, and these should always be heeded. A good rule of thumb is this – if you're not sure, don't get snap happy.

Dress Sense

We've talked about dress issues when visiting a Buddhist temple, but overall Sri Lanka doesn't have a very strict dress code away from religious sites. Despite this, if you are a woman in particular, unless you want to feel uncomfortable and attract unwanted attention, it's best to dress modestly, and not to flash the flesh. Shorts are fine, but not too short, as are dresses, and you can show your shoulders, provided you're not planning on heading to a temple. If you are, carry a light cardigan to cover you up.

Guys, despite the heat, it's not a good idea to walk around without a shirt on. This is a deeply spiritual and religious country, and despite its laid-back feel, you don't want to be causing offence.

In terms of topless sunbathing, or even nude sunbathing, it's basically not a good idea, and could land you in trouble with the law.

Romantic Issues

Okay, so if you're heading away with your significant other, the chances are that you want a little romantic time, and that is fine, provided you don't do it in public. In the tourist areas, holding hands isn't particularly frowned upon, but don't go around kissing or being overly touchy-feely, as this is considered bad etiquette. If you're in a nightclub, you do have a little more free rein, but it's probably best to just rein it in overall.

We have to mention that in Sri Lanka, same sex relationships are actually illegal.

How to Stay Connected With Loved Ones Back Home

The good news is that you shouldn't really struggle to find a good Wi-Fi connection when you're visiting Sri Lanka, provided you're in one of the main tourist areas. This means that you can easily stay in touch with your family and friends back home, with the online apps being the best way to do this, as well as the cheapest way.

Of course, you can do the old fashioned thing and pick up the phone, but this is likely to be costly, and you're probably going to get that really annoying delay on the line, which is never fun. For that reason, online is the way to go.

There are countless apps which help you stay in touch, just as they would be used when you're back home, including:

- Instagram
- Twitter
- Facebook, and Facebook Messenger
- WhatsApp
- Viber
- Tango

- Skype

These are the main ones, and more are being developed all the time. Can you remember the times when we only had the telephone (which was basic at best when overseas), and a pen and paper? Shudder at the thought! It used to take two weeks at best for a letter to return home, by which time you'd probably returned before it!

For safety reasons, do check in with someone back home on a regular basis, especially if you are travelling around the country. It's also a good idea to leave a copy of your rough itinerary with someone, and a copy of your passport, insurance details, visa paperwork, etc. Of course, hopefully nothing will ever be needed, but it pays to cover all bases.

As you can see, this chapter might have gone over some common sense issues, but a lot of it is quite pertinent to Sri Lanka itself. Knowing what you can do, what you can't do, and how to do it all in the right way, really does save you from not only embarrassment, but sometimes even worse situations.

Chapter 9: Red Tape, What to Pack, and What to Leave Behind

Don't you just love travel red tape? In fact, don't you just love red tape of any variety? It complicates matters, it means we need to research deeply, and it means we probably end up a bit paranoid, until we realise that we've been panicking for no

reason.

This is just a fact of life, unfortunately, and when it comes to visiting Sri Lanka, there is red tape to think about; not as much as some other countries, it has to be said, but there is tape that is red all the same.

This chapter is going to cover all of that red tape, so you don't have to be paranoid for a second longer. Just make sure you tick off every item we're going to talk about, and you're good to go. We're also going to tell you what you need to pack, and what you really don't. Whilst certain parts of Sri Lanka are a little basic, that doesn't mean that you can't buy toothpaste, so leave the kitchen sink at home!

Okay, on with the red tape.

Sri Lanka's Red Tape Issues You Need to Know About

When we talk about red tape, we're really talking about documentation. It really does depend on where you're from as to what amount of red tape you need to untangle, but overall, the guidelines are quite clear – thankfully!

There are things you need, that you cannot forget, and these are:

- Passport
- Visa
- Travel health insurance
- Driving licence and International Driving Permit (if you're planning on renting a car)

These are standard with every country the world over, but the rules do vary according to region. In terms of Sri Lanka's rules, this chapter will tell you everything you need to know, current and up to date.

Passport Issues

Your passport needs to be valid for six months or more after the date you are planning to leave the country and return home. So, if you're travelling to Sri Lanka on 1 August, and you're leaving on 1 September, your passport needs to be valid until the following March, just as an example. Even one month short of this six months' period can cause you problems, depending on the passport official checking your documentation on departure. You might get away with it, you might not, but the bottom line is that it's really not worth taking the risk. If your passport is due to expire before that, simply renew early.

Always keep your passport with you at all times, and if you are asked to present it by a police officer or any military personnel, do so without hesitation. It's a good idea to keep a photocopy of your passport in the safe back at the hotel, just in case of theft or loss.

Visa Issues

This particular section is going to be lengthy, so bear with us. This is because it is likely that all manner of nationalities could be reading this book, and therefore we have a lot of ground to cover! If you are at all concerned or confused, check with your consulate website for clarification of any issues.

The bottom line is that you DO need a visa to visit Sri Lanka, but this isn't a very formal one in most cases, but not all!

If you hold a passport from the following countries, you can obtain a free visa when you arrive at the airport in Colombo:

- Maldives
- Seychelles
- Singapore

This visa lasts for up to 30 days without any issue for passport holders from the Maldives and Singapore, and 60 days for nationals of the Seychelles. This visa can be extended for up to 150 and 90 days respectively, whilst in the country, and when done before the visa expires.

If you are from the following countries, you need to obtain a more formal visa:

- Cameroon
- Republic of the Congo & Democratic Republic of the Congo
- Cote d'Ivoire
- Egypt
- Gabon
- Ghana
- Guinea
- Guinea-Bissau
- Kenya
- Liberia
- Mali
- Nigeria
- Pakistan
- Sierra Leone
- Sudan
- Syria
- Uganda

In this case, you should contact your Embassy for instructions on how to begin the process. This process can be slow at certain times of the year, depending on demand, so do this ahead of time to avoid delay and disappointment.

Everyone else not mentioned is able to purchase a visa when they arrive at the airport in Colombo BUT they must first complete an online travel authorisation (ETA – Electronic Travel Authorisation). This can be done before travel, or at the airport, but it is strongly advised to do it beforehand, to avoid any delays or issues when you arrive at a busy airport, in the stifling heat!

The cost of this visa currently is $15 for nationals of Bangladesh, Bhutan, India, the Maldives, Nepal, and Pakistan, and $30 for everyone else who is not mentioned, aside from those on the formal visa list above.

The Electronic Travel Authorisation (ETA)

We'll have a separate section for this as there are a few things you need to know, to ensure you don't have any other issues, aside from it being a bit hot when you arrive!

- Valid for three months upon approval – approval is usually instant, so if you do it too far in front, you're going to run out whilst you're there
- You can enter Sri Lanka on two occasions during this three months' period of time
- You can stay for up to 30 days maximum on both occasions – 60 days in total, but not all in one go
- If you want to stay for longer than 30 days without leaving the country and re-entering, you can apply for an extension whilst you're in the country, which can be granted up to 90 days on both entry occasions
- It is possible to be turned down for this authorisation, and in that case, you will need to contact the Sri Lanka Overseas Mission for help and advice – the 24 hour assistance telephone number is 0094 719 967 888
- When filling in the details on your authorisation application, be very careful when entering the passport document number. If one digit is out, you may have an issue when you arrive at the airport. This should exactly match your passport

Whilst this visa information may sound complicated, you simply need to find your particular country of origin amongst the list and then follow the information to the letter.

Travel Health Insurance Issues

If you travel without adequate travel health insurance, you are basically playing Russian roulette with your life. This is a must have, and you should never attempt to go anywhere without it. Not only is your luggage at risk, i.e. if it gets damaged or lost, you're not really going to have a claim to put in, but your health in the event of a problem could be in grave danger. If you don't have insurance, you have the price tag to pay, and if you can't pay it?

Difficulties, very big difficulties.

For that reason, travel health insurance is something you need to get well ahead of time. There are a few rules in terms of finding this:

- Always declare pre-existing medical conditions at the time of arranging your cover – failure to do so could mean that your policy is null and void in the event of a claim
- Shop around for the best policy – a price comparison site is always a good bet, but check the fine print very carefully. A cheap policy might be good for your wallet, but it might not be great in terms of what it does, and more often than not, doesn't cover
- If you are going backpacking, and visiting several countries, with Sri Lanka, just one of them, you need special insurance, which we will cover in a bit more detail shortly
- If you are going to be doing any extreme sports during your time away, perhaps bungee jumping or you fancy risking your sanity by jumping out of a plane, then you need to make sure that your policy is going to cover you, and that means usually purchasing an add

on

- Check the excess costs, i.e. how much it actually costs for you to make a claim. The more you pay for your policy, the lower the excess costs will usually be, and vice versa
- Once you have purchased your policy, keep the emails in your inbox (in case you somehow lose the paperwork), store the emergency claim number in your phone contacts, and print out a copy of the certificate and finer details, to take with you in your hand luggage – this is what you will need to present to the hospital, or the airline, should you need to make a claim

Backpacking Insurance

We need to make a special mention towards backpacking insurance, because this is a little different. Most standard travel insurance policies cover you for one destination, for one trip. The exact time constraints on this should be checked out, because they will vary from company to company, but overall, you will have to enter in the country you're going to be visiting, in order to obtain the policy. Now, when you're backpacking, you aren't just visiting one country, but several, and that makes life a little difficult.

Fear not however, because if you are backpacking your way around Asia, for instance, and Sri Lanka is a beautiful stop on your journey, then there are special backpacking insurance policies out there, which will cover you for your journey. You will need to search for this online, because the price of the policy will be determined by your age, any pre-existing medical conditions you may have, any adventure activities you're planning on doing whilst you're away, and exactly where it is that you're going to be

going during your trip, e.g. the region. For instance, if you were to be travelling across the Middle East currently, the cost of your trip may be higher than when travelling across Europe.

Backpacker insurance usually covers you for around one year in duration, and it often includes a clause where you can go back home for a visit once during this time, for a set amount of days. If you go over this, your policy is null and void.

Check out your insurance options very carefully before making a decision, because when heading to any country which is far-flung, which for the most part Sri Lanka will be, you need to be safe in the knowledge that you're covered for all eventualities.

Driving Licence Issues

We did cover driving licence issues in our 'how to get around' chapter, but for the sake of completion, and to keep all documentation needs in one place, let's sum it up again.

We know that you need an International Driving Permit to be able to drive in Sri Lanka, and that this needs to be accredited by the Sri Lankan authorities when you arrive. For that reason, before you travel you need to make sure that you take your actual driving licence with you (card and paper copy, if applicable), as well as obtaining your International Driving Permit and taking that with you too.

Currency and How to Carry it

Another red tape issue, in terms of safety more than anything else, is currency.

Whilst in the big cities, especially Colombo, you won't have an issue finding an ATM to withdraw cash, meaning you don't have to take out too much at any one time, but if you're planning on going off the beaten track, this might not be a hugely available option for you.

We know that carrying large amounts of cash on you is not a good idea in terms of safety, so how exactly can you carry your cash safely and sensibly, to ensure you're not going to run out, or become a crime target?

Remember to tell your bank that you're going to be using your debit and credit cards overseas, because some visitors do experience temporary blocks to their cards if they don't do this. The official term is a 'travel marker', and you simply need to call your bank and tell them of your travel plans; a note will then be put on your account, so the fraud department don't suspect that someone other than you has got you card in their possession and is using it for other means. If you don't do this, and you do have a block on your account, you're going to have to try and call the bank from Sri Lanka itself, which isn't always easy, and then answer all manner of security questions, which can be difficult when you're stressed and under pressure. Save yourself the hassle.

It's not a good idea to change too much cash all at once, because when you leave the country, it is illegal to take Sri Lankan Rupees with you. This is because this isn't an internationally recognised currency, and can only be used in the country anyway. If you change cash at a money changing office, you will be given a certificate, and you will need to keep this, as you may be asked to show it when you leave the country to go back home.

When you arrive in Colombo, take out enough money to last you for a few days, which shouldn't be too much anyway. Budgeting it the way forward here, and you can repeat this process every few days, or every week, whenever you run out. In terms of carrying it, it's a good idea to purchase a money belt, and keep your cash on you in this way. If you have it in your bag, and your bag is stolen, that means all your cash is gone too.

If you are staying in a large resort or city however, you can use your cards to pay at large restaurants, hotels, and bars, so in this regard, you may not need to take too much cash out of the machine, or exchange it, anyway.

What to Pack and What to Leave Behind

We've covered red tape now, so you can stop yawning! Seriously though, it might be a boring subject to cover, but it is one that needs to be thoroughly done, otherwise your dream trip to Sri Lanka may just turn into a nightmare.

All that over and done with, let's talk about the fun stuff now – what to pack, and what to leave at home!

We talked earlier on in the book about the weather, and for that reason, your packing requirements are quite a mixed bag, regardless of when you are visiting. It can rain at any time, a little or a lot, and if you're moving around the country, you need to have all bases covered in terms of not forgetting something important.

You don't need to take all your belongings with you, because there are many shops in Sri Lanka! This is not at third world country, you can buy things here!

It's easy to want to take all your clothes, or everything you might have bought in readiness for your trip, but the bottom line is that you don't really need to. If you're backpacking or moving around, lightweight luggage is key, especially on public transport, and even more so when trying to cram yourself and your bags into a Tuk-Tuk!

Let's explore those packing needs in a bit more detail – it's time to be ruthless!

What to Pack For Sri Lanka

Let's assume that you're visiting for a standard two week break. If you're going for longer, you will need

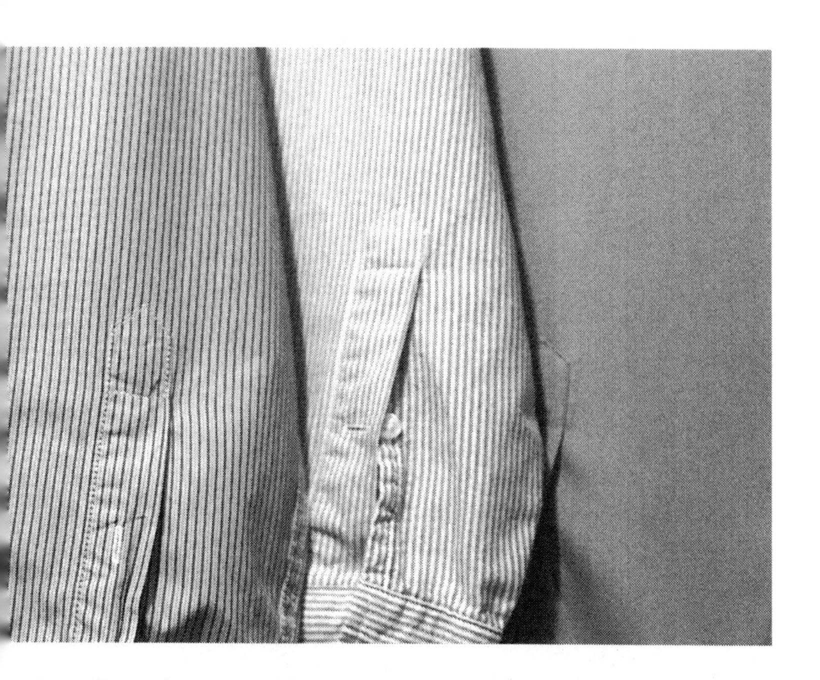

to adjust the quantities here to your needs, and if you're going for just a week, then you need to do some halving.

This is what you definitely need in your bag:

- Toiletries – This should include toothbrush, toothpaste, hand sanitiser, deodorant, wet wipes, shower gel, shampoo, conditioner – that's it! Everything else is a luxury, and if you really need it, you can buy it there. You also don't need to take two of everything, one is sufficient!
- Suntan lotion
- Mosquito repellent
- A small first aid kit - Including antiseptic cream, painkillers, tablets for an upset stomach, plasters, any medications you regularly take (keep them in your hand luggage), a pair of tweezers, bite or sting cream – Again, everything else you can buy there
- A thin, lightweight rain jacket – Anything too thick or heavy is going

to make you too hot, or weigh you down, you just need something ultra-thin, preferably which can roll up into a small bundle in your bag, for just in case moments

- Device chargers and plug adapters – If you can purchase a charger which is multi-purpose, e.g. has a plug end for all your devices, this will save you plentiful room
- Underwear – Clean every day, of course!
- Nightwear – Three pairs of pyjamas, or night-shirts should be enough
- Sandals – For those obligatory beach days. One pair of flip flops should be enough, as these are certainly plentiful in shops on the island. If you are visiting a resort and you want to go out in the evening, you can take an extra pair for those occasions
- Lightweight trainers for outdoor walking – Make sure these are made of a breathable fabric, but which are waterproof at the same time
- A cardigan for visiting temples, to cover arms
- Ladies – a long skirt or a pair of lightweight pants for covering legs when visiting temples. Also, a pair of lightweight pants for the guys when doing the same thing
- Swimwear – Two sets should be plentiful
- Beach towel – One is enough!
- Day time clothes – For this you need to think mix and match, and remember that you can wash your clothes quite easily in hotels. Think lightweight, breathable materials, so we're talking shorts, cotton clothing, and certainly not jeans
- Evening clothes – If you're visiting a resort you'll want to go out in the evening and you'll need dressy clothes for that. Again, don't go OTT, you can mix and match here too. Ladies, think maxi dresses and jewellery with flats, and guys, think linen pants and a shirt, for a

really casual look

That's really is. Honestly, you don't need anything else. If you pack too much, you're just weighing yourself down, and what's the point in that?

Now let's look at what you definitely don't need.

What to Leave at Home

Sri Lanka is a vibrant and fun island, but it is not a party-mad island, so ladies, leave those sky-high shoes at home, and guys, forget about those dress pants and blazers. You need to think about casual clothing, cool fabrics, and items that you can mix and match.

The chilled out feel on Sri Lanka will have you wanting to live a more minimalistic lifestyle pretty quickly, and it's also easy to purchase clothing in the big cities too – linens and cottons are very cheap and you can give yourself a makeover for a fraction of the price you could do at home.

To give you an idea of what you don't need however, these items need to remain in your closet:

- Heels
- Heavy, dress shoes
- Jeans
- Coats
- Any clothing which features social, political or religious slogans – You're best sticking to simple items
- Anything which features Buddha – We talked about this earlier, but any accessories or clothing which features Buddha will cause extreme offence, and could land you in trouble
- Guide books – We're biased of course, but simply download this book onto your tablet or smartphone, and you're not only saving space, but you're getting the best

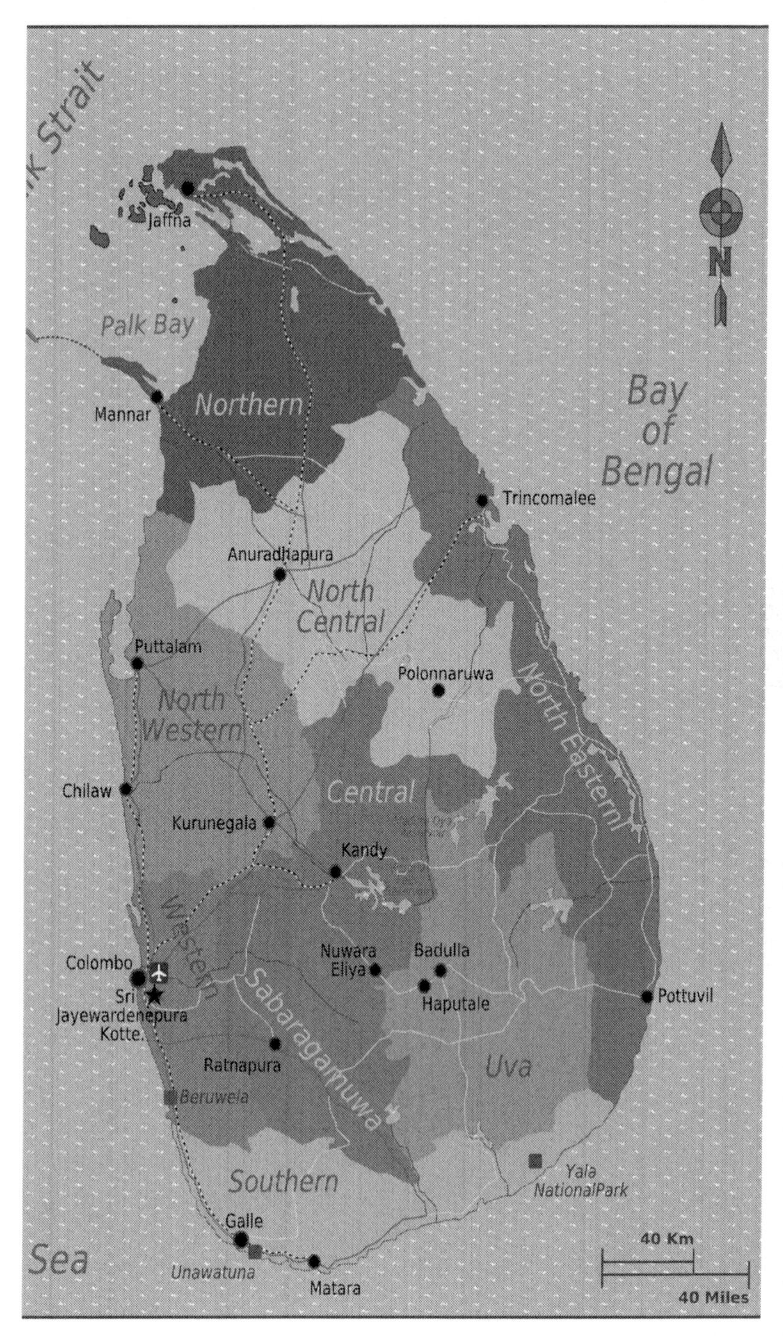
Palk Strait
Jaffna
Palk Bay
Mannar
Northern
Bay of Bengal
Trincomalee
Anuradhapura
North Central
Puttalam
Polonnaruwa
North Eastern
North Western
Chilaw
Central
Kurunegala
Kandy
Western
Nuwara Eliya
Badulla
Colombo
Sri Jayewardenepura Kotte
Haputale
Pottuvil
Sabaragamuwa
Ratnapura
Uva
Beruwela
Southern
Yala NationalPark
Galle
40 Km
Sea
Unawatuna
Matara
40 Miles
N

information too!

- Hairdryer – Most hotels will have one, and with the heat, your hair is going to dry fast anyway; save yourself the space

As you can see, a vacation in Sri Lanka doesn't require a huge amount of clothing, nor does it need six suitcases! You can easily get away with basics, and we just mentioned, the chilled out vibe really isn't at all focused on appearance, and much more focused on having a good time, and enjoying everything beautiful which surrounds you.

The downside is that the varied nature of the island (if you can call it a downside), means that your day pack needs to contain a few varied items too! For instance, you can be on a jungle trek in the morning, and lazing on a beach in the afternoon! You can be in the city first thing, and then venture to a temple at lunch time, before deciding you want to enjoy the last few hours of sun on the beach in the late afternoon. Of course, it may rain, and that might mean you need a lightweight rain jacket, whilst also a pair of flip flops and some suncream!

The answer? Pack for every eventuality, but do it in a streamlined manner!

Conclusion – Ready and Raring to go?

We have come to the end of our journey together. Do not shed a tear, because now the good stuff can start – it's time for us to bid you goodbye, and wave you off into the sunset, ready to begin your Sri Lankan adventure.

Never feel that you are alone however, because we may not be there in person, but we certainly are in spirit – you can dib into this book again at any time, whenever you need a little inspiration or guidance. It's unlikely that you're going to read the entirety of this book and remember it all, but our interactive contents list is easy for you to find exactly what you're looking for on the go, allowing you to jump straight to the information that you need.

The hope is that by reading this book you have developed a real passion and excitement for you upcoming trip, and if you were on the fence at the beginning, that you're now converted and ready to book that dream trip of yours.

You don't have to be an epic adventurer to really explore and enjoy Sri Lanka, you can simply want to head to a beach resort and enjoy a few guided excursions – it doesn't matter how you explore it, what matters is that you see it and enjoy it for all that it is meant to be.

The history, the wildlife, nature, the people, customs, serenity, peace, the beauty, and the spirituality of this island really does provide visitors with a true glimpse into the special and unique way of life that happens every single day. Being able to see this for yourself is something truly once in a lifetime, and whether you're visiting as part of a meditation retreat, or you're simply wanting to visit the elephants, the underwater residents of the Indian Ocean, and enjoy the beautiful scenery, the bottom line is that you will certainly want to return.

Make sure that you cover all sections in the red tape chapter, to ensure that there are no concerns or problems when you arrive, and always follow our health and safety advice to the letter. Basically, as long as you keep your brain in your head, and don't leave it at the airport departure desk, you're going to have a safe and happy experience. Sri Lanka has had a troubled past, and of course it's not perfect, but is anywhere these days? With the rise of international terrorism, crime, and other dark and dismal subjects, we have forgotten that the world is there to be explored to the max. There are few destinations on the planet that offer such a unique experience as Sri Lanka, and it is a generally very safe destination too.

So, it's time to draw up your itinerary, check out what it is that you really want to see when you visit, think about the delicious food you're going to try, and how many cocktails you're considering enjoying on your first night, and to truly look forward to visiting one of the most stunning destinations on the planet.

We're jealous, truly we are!

Picture credits

https://www.flickr.com/https://www.flickr.com/photos/125463433@N02/
https://www.flickr.com/photos/mal-b/
https://www.flickr.com/photos/ronsaunders47/
https://www.flickr.com/photos/dronepicr
https://www.flickr.com/photos/mckaysavage/
https://www.flickr.com/photos/AndrewFysh
https://www.flickr.com/photos/JanArendtsz
https://www.flickr.com/photos/cat_collector
https://www.flickr.com/photos/AlexisGravel
https://www.flickr.com/photos/AndreasKretschmer
https://www.flickr.com/photos/MichaelTheis
https://www.flickr.com/photos/MalB
https://www.flickr.com/photos/MichalBocek
https://www.flickr.com/photos/RuthHartnup
https://www.flickr.com/photos/AaronGoodman
https://www.flickr.com/photos/AmilaTennakoon

Printed in Great Britain
by Amazon